NUMBERS DO WONDERS

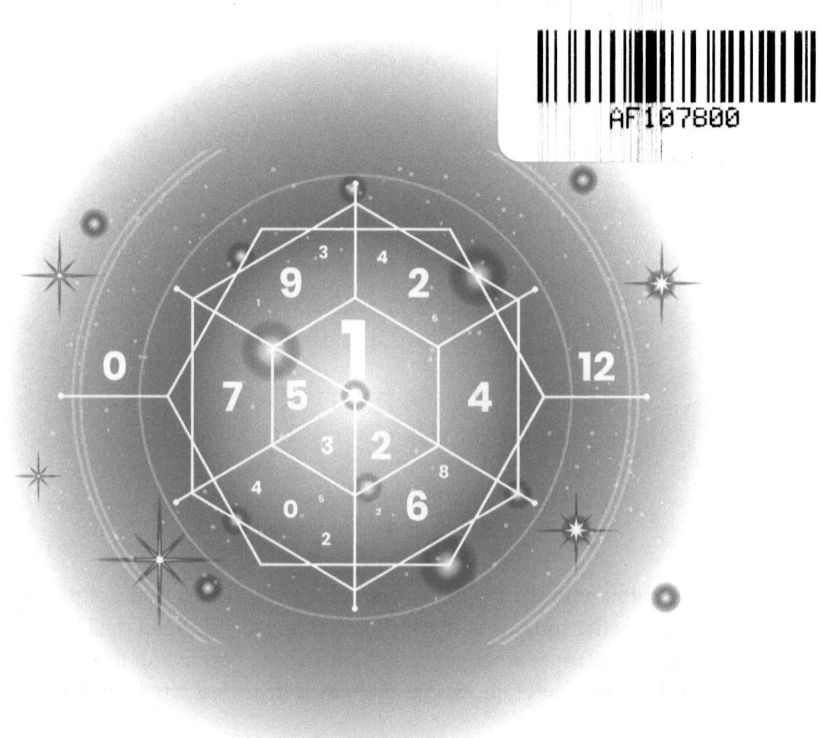

Jhhilmil M Shah

Chennai • Bangalore

CLEVER FOX PUBLISHING
Chennai, India

Published by CLEVER FOX PUBLISHING 2024
Copyright © Jhhilmil M Shah 2024

All Rights Reserved.
ISBN: 978-93-56489-76-9

This book has been published with all reasonable efforts taken to make the material error-free after the consent of the author. No part of this book shall be used, reproduced in any manner whatsoever without written permission from the author, except in the case of brief quotations embodied in critical articles and reviews.

The Author of this book is solely responsible and liable for its content including but not limited to the views, representations, descriptions, statements, information, opinions and references ["Content"]. The Content of this book shall not constitute or be construed or deemed to reflect the opinion or expression of the Publisher or Editor. Neither the Publisher nor Editor endorse or approve the Content of this book or guarantee the reliability, accuracy or completeness of the Content published herein and do not make any representations or warranties of any kind, express or implied, including but not limited to the implied warranties of merchantability, fitness for a particular purpose. The Publisher and Editor shall not be liable whatsoever for any errors, omissions, whether such errors or omissions result from negligence, accident, or any other cause or claims for loss or damages of any kind, including without limitation, indirect or consequential loss or damage arising out of use, inability to use, or about the reliability, accuracy or sufficiency of the information contained in this book.

PREFACE

"*N*umber Rules The Universe"- Pythagoras. They actually do…

I was not aware until I ventured into numerology how numbers affected and impacted everything in one's life. Prior to being exposed to the mystic realm of numbers, I was only exposed to subjects that involved numbers, the majority of which I found difficult to get into (like mathematics), but even in spite of this, I understood the significance of numbers because they form the foundation of all sciences.

Numbers consciously and subconsciously play a very important role in one's life, even before the person is born. All the calculations are made in order for the mother to become pregnant, and when everything lines up, it happens.

As a numerologist, I come into contact with people from all walks of life, age groups, backgrounds, and religions on a daily basis. They are generally divided into two categories- the aware and the unaware. This leads to a further difference in their mindsets and behaviours, as they think and behave very differently in terms of their way of looking at life, its challenges, and their way of handling them. People who are aware have clarity on the path they need to follow to come out of a situation.

I would be honest to admit I was in the second category before venturing into numerology and before understanding the power of numbers.

Let me tell you a little bit about me to help you understand the magic that numbers have created in my life. I was born on the 8th of July, and life has been a rollercoaster for me since my birth; in fact, my mother's life has been especially challenging. I was a rebellious child, strong-headed, affectionate, considerate, and driven.

One thing that was unusual about me was that I was very accident-prone. I come from the small town of Jamshedpur (the same place where Ratan Tata, my idol, comes from). Education, though it is our birthright, is not easy for a girl, especially coming from a Gujarati family where girls are married off once they turn 18. My mom was married at the age of 19. But I, being number 8(which you will know about in the book), was a person who would not give up on her dreams and was very ambitious from the very beginning. I fought with the family, demanding higher education outside of Jamshedpur, as the place does not have good colleges after the 12th standard.

I landed in Pune, and my journey started in the year 2000 (which was my personal year number 8 again) outside of my comfort zone. It took a lot of courage to come out of my comfort bubble, yet a pinch of excitement rushed toward me as I was exposed to the real world. I never knew how numbers were playing their magic to make me reach where I was meant to be. Magic began, but only after a lot of testing for miracles to happen.

I had taken up French as my second language in college (Symbiosis College of Arts and Commerce), and at the end of my first year, I was selected to be sent to France for a cultural exchange programme.

Happiness knew no bounds, as I was the first in my entire extended family of the Shah Clan to be sent abroad. It was fate, even though I didn't even have a passport, to learn that I would be travelling immediately to France in less than 45 days. I was over the moon to be bestowed with such an opportunity.

I was the first from the family but also the last batch from college, as 9/11 (the Twin Tower attack) happened the same year. An incident that shook the world and had a lot of numerological ties. Flight 11 hit the World Trade Centre. which looks like 11, had 110 stories each, New York (the 11th state in the Union), and 911 is also the number that one calls in case of any emergency. A total of September 11, 2001, comes to the number 14, which is a karmic number. All this can't be a coincidence, or it can be if you still don't believe in numerology.

After completing my post-graduation in mass communication and topping the course, I moved to Mumbai to work in media. My journey in the television industry started in 2006 (which was the Dog Chinese year). I was also born in the dog year, so another number got attached in 2006, which totals to the number 8.

I struggled for over 15 years without realizing the purpose of my life, until numerology entered my life.

Fast forward to 2019. The world changed, and so did my life. The worst year of my life affected all areas. I lost my job, my partner left me because of caste issues and his family did not agree, my mom was diagnosed with ovarian cancer, and I was locked all alone in COVID-19 in my house in Gurgaon. I was broken and shattered with no hope to live when God sent angels into my life as friends, keeping me alive.

In 2020, Numerology entered and gave answers to all my questions and solutions to all my problems. I had found treasure in numerology. Passion turned into a profession as it changed my life in 360 degrees.

I had mentioned I was prone to accidents, not because I was careless but because my name number came to an anti-number. After changing the spelling of my name from Jhilmil to Jhhilmil, a tiny bit of correction led to the beginning of magic in my life.

With an overwhelming desire to return the favours the universe had bestowed on me, I began teaching numerology. It is one of the biggest mysteries solved and used by millions across the globe to predict and create magic, and this gave rise to the book - 'Numbers Do Wonders'.

Connect with us @ Metavalley

CONTENTS

- Introduction 2
- Concepts Of Numerology 5
- Pure Numbers 7
- Compound Numbers 9
- Root Number 11
- Life Path Number 14
- Numerology and Nine Planets (Navagraha) of Astrology 17
- Colors and Numbers 20
- Days of the week and Nine numbers 22
- Zodiac Numbers 25
- Karmic Numbers 30
- Master Numbers 33
- Compatibility Of Numbers/ Relationship between numbers 35
- Careers and Numerology 38
- Health and Numerology 41
- Name Number 43
- Remedies for Numbers 46
  - Elemental Remedies 47
  - Yantras 48
  - Mantras 49
  - Beej Mantras 50
  - Lucky Gemstone 51
- Lucky Vehicle Number 53

- ✶ Lucky Mobile Number 55
- ✶ Lucky House Number 57
- ✶ The Number 1 59
- ✶ The Number 2 73
- ✶ The Number 3 86
- ✶ The Number 4 98
- ✶ The Number 5 117
- ✶ The Number 6 134
- ✶ The Number 7 152
- ✶ The Number 8 166
- ✶ The Number 9 182

Conclusion *195*

INTRODUCTION

INTRODUCTION

> *"Numbers have life; they are not just symbols on paper."*
> – **Shakuntala Devi**

*W*ell, if you are someone who believes in energy, you will also believe in numerology, and numbers are nothing but different energies. The study of numerology shows the enigmatic connections between numbers, letters, and patterns.

There are various schools or types of numerology. The most popular ones are:-

- Chaldean Numerology.
- Kabbalah Numerology.
- Western/Pythagorean Numerology.
- Chinese Numerology.

Each form has its strengths and limitations. So, the one I follow is a combination of all, which gives me accurate results.

Numerology can act like a mirror, which sees through and reflects not only your external aspects but can also reflect your internal desires, goals, dilemmas, and dreams.

Numerology is vast, intense, and an ocean of understanding human life, the patterns, and the consequences.

Writing about only the nine numbers will take at least nine books, but I and my 15 certified students decided to put the crux in this one book about the nine numbers, revealing the different dimensions attached to it.

Within the pages of this book, we invite you to embark on a fascinating journey into the profound world of numerology.

Now it is time to get into the depths of each of the nine numbers. Numerology is extremely potent and has connections to nearly everything in the cosmos. The nine numbers have significance in various aspects of life. Each number is going to help you comprehend everything about the person connected with the number.

This book aims to help you understand the power of numbers, its impact on your life, and use numerology to make life better, achieve financial abundance, have the best of relationships, and make the right decisions at the right time.

Let's begin the journey into the world of nine numbers and their influence on human life.

CONCEPTS OF NUMEROLOGY

*T*here are more than 200 concepts in numerology through which one can understand and predict a person. Although numerology is a mysterious study that dates back thousands of years, its popularity has recently grown and continues to do so daily.

Numerology is all about understanding the meanings and energies associated with numbers. Each number holds unique qualities and vibrations that can influence different aspects of our lives..Numerology is a means to investigate the deeper relationships between numbers and life occurrences; it's not simply about mathematics.

To begin with, the first concept is about the intensity of numbers.

PURE NUMBERS

*N*umerology goes well beyond the nine numbers, but when these numbers are present directly, they are known as pure numbers and have the maximum strength and qualities of the number.

So, everyone who is born between the 1st and the 9th of any month is said to be born as pure numbers and will reflect the maximum strength and qualities of the numbers.

Similarly, when you see the number between 1 and 9 coming directly into your life, anywhere will have the strongest quality and impact of the number. For instance, football player Cristiano Ronaldo with jersey number 7 will have a stronger impact with jersey number 7 than Rob Holding (Arsenal), who wears jersey number 16, which also adds up to 7. So people born on the 1st of any month are more of a leader than someone born on the 28th, which is also number 1.

COMPOUND NUMBERS

*A*ll the numbers from 10 upwards become compound numbers and have a meaning of their own. Single numbers denote what you appear to be in the eyes of others, while double or compound numbers show the hidden influences that play a role behind the scenes and, in some mysterious way, often predict the future more precisely.

Now, single numbers can convey a person's temperament, traits, strengths and weaknesses, and how the outside world views him.

But the compound numbers can talk about the hidden secrets, the inner desires, and the inner self, so the compound numbers can open a whole new dimension to understanding a person.

So, people born between the 10th and 31st of any month are born as compound numbers and have characteristics of both the numbers they have in their date of birth. Someone born on the 23rd of any month will display qualities of number 2 and number 3.

Understanding compound numbers can take one to the depths of the ocean of numerology and knowing and predicting a person.

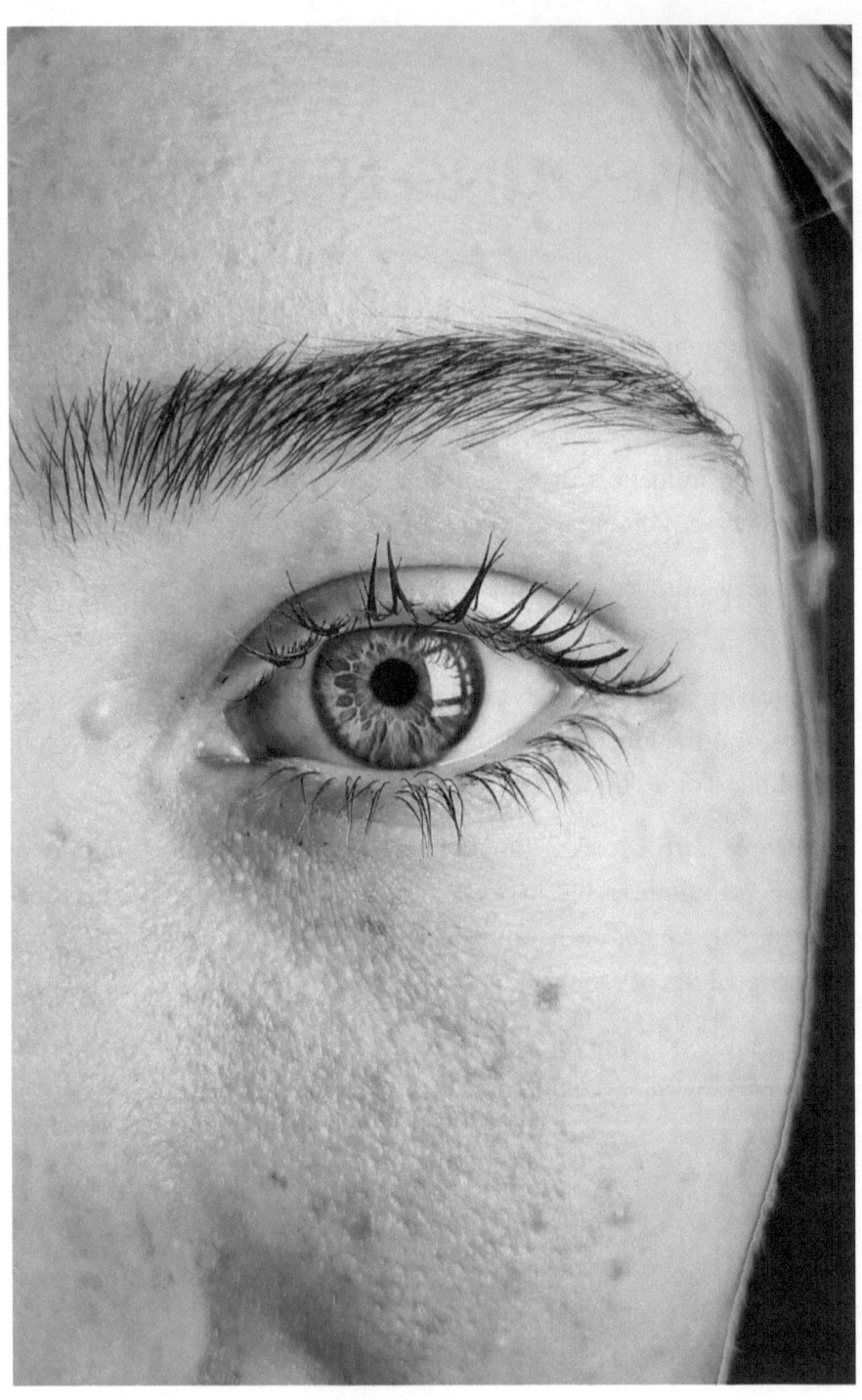

ROOT NUMBER

*I*n numerology, a root/psychic number is **a number that governs a person's characteristics and personality**. A root number is a single number based on the date of birth.

If a person is born on a pure number, then that date becomes the person's root number, and if the person is born after the 9th of any month, then it is calculated by adding a person's birthday.

For example, if someone is born on March 22, their root/psychic number is 4 (2 + 2 = 4).

A person's root number can accurately characterize them. To put it plainly, the root number is the response to the query, "Who are you?"

The Root number for people born on the 1st, 10th, 19th or 28th is 1.

The Root number for people born on the 2nd, 11th, 20th or 29th is 2.

The Root number for people born on the 3rd, 12th, 21st or 30th is 3.

The Root number for people born on the 4th, 13th, 22nd or 31st is 4.

The Root number for people born on the 5th, 14th, or 23rd is 5.

The Root number for people born on the 6th, 15th, or 24th is 6.

The Root number for people born on the 7th, 16th, or 25th is 7.

The Root number for people born on the 8th, 17th, or 26th is 8.

The Root number for people born on the 9th, 18th, or 27th is 9.

Each root number creates a different and unique character, and this concept is used to understand how the world sees you. It reveals your identity, including your strengths, weaknesses, talents, and ambitions. The root number rules one's life until the age of 35.

LIFE PATH NUMBER

LIFE PATH NUMBER

One of the most important numbers in numerology, also known as the life path number or destiny number, is derived from a person's birthdate. As the name suggests, it is the number that defines or shapes your destiny, your purpose of life, and the number that talks about why you are here.

The life path number is the number that represents the path that an individual is destined to take in their life, revealing their innate characteristics, strengths, challenges, and potential life experiences.

If you understand SWOT analysis, which is (Strengths, Weaknesses, Opportunities, and Threats), then the root number talks about the first two, i.e., strengths and weaknesses, whereas the life path number talks about the last two, i.e., opportunities and threats.

The life path number is calculated using the person's date of birth, which is reduced to a single-digit number.

Let's calculate the Life path number of

Ratan Naval Tata

(born 28, December 1937) -

Date format used in India - DD/MM/YYYY (28/12/1937)

Your Life Path Number is derived by taking the sum of all the numbers in your birthdate and reducing it to a single digit.

Life Path Number -28/12/1937

2+8+1+2+1+9+3+7= 33

33=3+3=6.

Life Path Number= 6

A lot of forms of numerology do not reduce the numbers 11, 22, and 33 to a single digit, as these numbers are considered master numbers, and these numbers hold a special place in numerology and are more powerful than other compound numbers.

Every life path number possesses a unique blend of positive and negative qualities, but you are ultimately in charge of the outcomes.

Life unfolds before you, offering numerous chances to harness the opportunities and threats associated with your life path number.

You decide which path to follow, whether one that is easy and wrong or one that is difficult and right, regardless of the circumstances.

Each experience becomes a lesson, a stepping stone towards realizing your fullest, most awesome self.

Like the Root number, which rules the first half of one's life until the age of 35, the life path number rules the second half post 35 years until the last day of one's life. Knowing the life path and understanding the potential is like uncovering a hidden treasure.

I often say that numerology is like a lotus; with every concept, a different petal begins to reveal a different aspect of an individual.

NUMEROLOGY AND NINE PLANETS (NAVAGRAHA) OF ASTROLOGY

*I*n Hinduism and Hindu astrology, the "Navagraha" refers to a group of nine celestial entities and deities that exert influence over human life on Earth. The term "Navagraha" is derived from the Sanskrit words "Nava," meaning "nine," and "graha," signifying "planet" or "celestial force."

These nine constituents of the Navagraha include the Sun, the Moon, the planets Mercury, Venus, Mars, Jupiter, and Saturn, as well as the two lunar nodes - Rahu and Ketu. Rahu and Ketu are considered shadow planets and do not rule over any zodiac sign because they are not physical planets. In astrology, there is a sloka, which goes as,

अंगारकफलं केतो राहोरप्यर्कजस्य वै ।

(Angarkphalam Keto Rahorpyarkjasya vee)

The meaning of the above Sanskrit sloka is that Ketu is similar to Mars, and Rahu is similar to Saturn in giving effects.

The nine numbers are connected to a particular planet based on the similarity of the qualities of the number and planet.

Number	Planets	Planets
1	Sun	Surya/Ravi
2	Moon	Chandrama/Somay
3	Jupiter	Guru/Brihaspati
4	North- Node	Rahu
5	Mercury	Buddh
6	Venus	Shukr
7	South- Node	Ketu
8	Saturn	Shani
9	Mars	Mangal

These nine planets and the nine numbers are closely connected to each other. Both of them possess distinct attributes, energies, and qualities that shape the individual born under their influence.

So, when numbers are connected to planets, they also get connected to all concepts of numerology. This concept of numbers connected to planets is used to understand a person better. As in numerology, your ruling planet is the planet connected to your root number.

For example, If you were born on the 28th of any month,

2+8=10=1+0=1

The root number is 1, and the planet connected to number 1 is the Planet Sun. So, The Sun becomes your ruling planet as per numerology, which is going to impact and define your nature, qualities, habits, strengths, and challenges.

COLORS AND NUMBERS

COLORS AND NUMBERS

*S*ince different variations of colors have distinct effects on our brains, colors can be considered to have a notable impact on us and can influence our state of mind and innate nature.

Colors are also connected to numbers in numerology through different concepts. One connection is through feng-shui, and the other is through the nine planets of astrology, or the Navagraha.

Each color has a positive and negative impact on us. For example, red is connected to energy, passion, and love on the positive side, but on the negative side, it is connected to aggression, anger, and danger.

When studied and used according to numerology, colours can help bring an abundance of health, wealth, and happiness.

Every color possesses distinct qualities and attributes in numerology. Hence, it is crucial to showcase the appropriate color that aligns with your fortunate number.

Numerology offers various avenues to integrate your lucky color. This can involve incorporating it into the food you consume, the clothing and accessories you wear, or the statement pieces you use to adorn your home.

DAYS OF THE WEEK AND NINE NUMBERS

Monday

Tuesday

Wednesday

Thursday

Friday

Saturday

Sunday

DAYS OF THE WEEK AND NINE NUMBERS

From the nine planets of the Navagraha, seven are named after the planets in the solar system and correspond with the names of the seven days in the week of the Hindu calendar.

Also, we learned that Rahu is like Saturn and Ketu is like Mars; they share the same weekdays, respectively. No specific days are assigned to Rahu and Ketu.

Since the nine numbers are connected to the nine planets, or Navagraha, we have one number connected to each day of the week.

Number	Planets	Day Of The Week
1	Sun	Sunday
2	Moon	Monday
3	Jupiter	Thursday
4	Rahu	Saturday
5	Mercury	Wednesday
6	Venus	Friday
7	Ketu	Tuesday
8	Saturn	Saturday
9	Mars	Tuesday

This connection is also used when one knows the day of birth, which will in turn bring in the energies of the number connected to that day. This affects them so strongly that even if the person does not have the number connected to the day of birth, the person will still show strong characteristics of the number connected to the day.

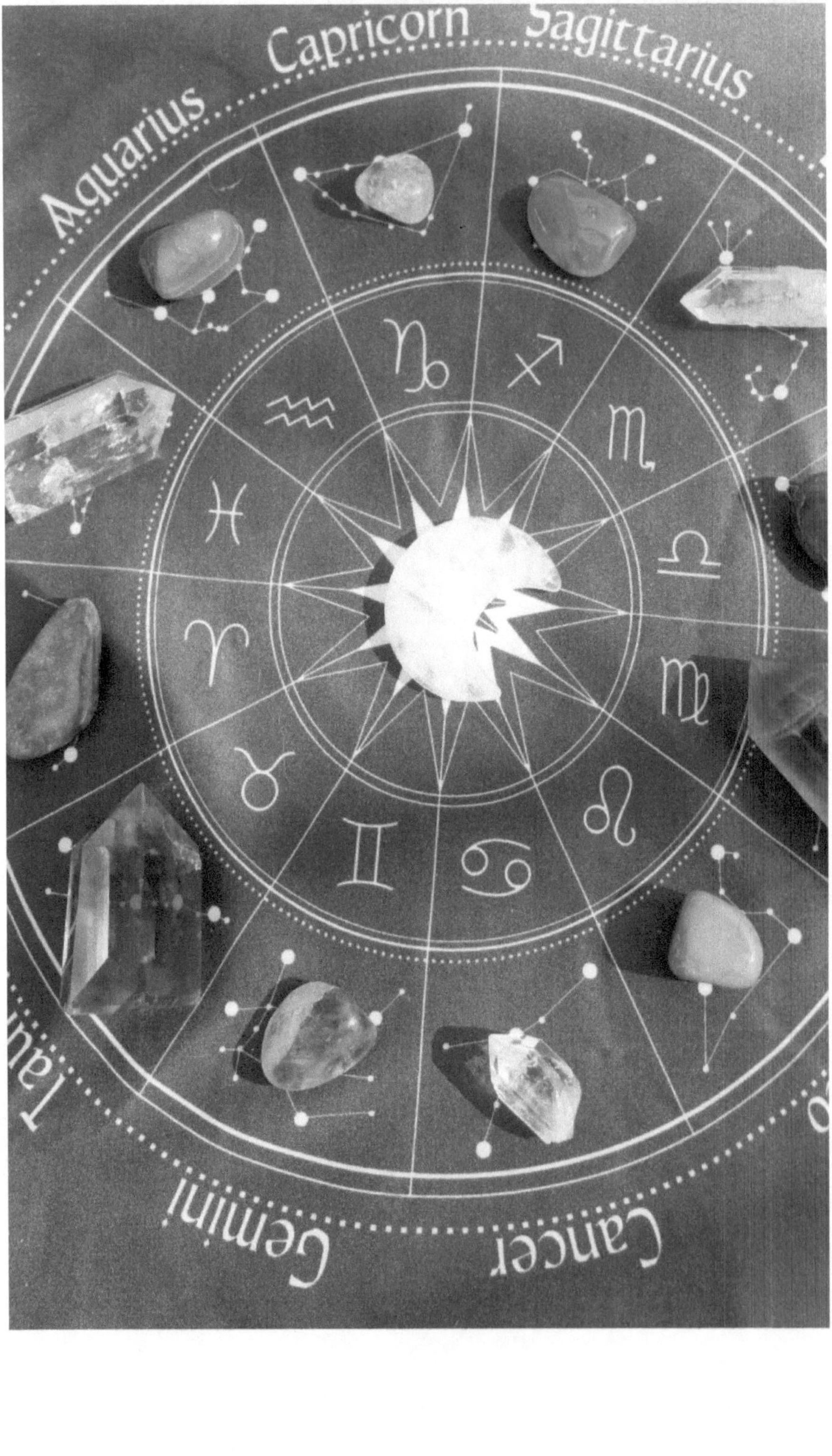
Aquarius
Capricorn
Sagittarius
Gemini
Cancer

ZODIAC NUMBERS

Though Astrology and Numerology are two different forms of occult sciences, they are closely connected. I realised this connection when I started studying numerology. Everything an astrologer predicted through the horoscope was quite similar to the predictions made by numerology.

Where astrology is the study of the impact of the planets and stars on human life, numerology primarily deals with the extensive study of numbers and how they are correlated to the actual circumstances of life.

We learned before how the nine planets (Navagraha) are connected to the nine numbers. Let's now understand how the 12 zodiac signs are also connected to numbers.

There are two systems to understand the zodiac - Western astrology and Vedic astrology.

No	English Names (Signs)	Hindu Names (Rashi)	English Name	Symbol	Sidereal zodiac (2011) (Indian-Niryana)	Tropical zodiac (2011) (Western-Sayana)
1	Aries	Mesh	The Ram	♈	15 April -15 May	21 March – 20 April
2	Taurus	Vrish	The Bull	♉	16 May -15 June	21 April – 21 May
3	Gemini	Mithun	The Twins	♊	16 June -15 July	22 May – 21 June
4	Cancer	Karka	The Crab	♋	16 July -15 Aug.	22 June – 22 July
5	Leo	Simha	The Lion	♌	16 Aug. -15 Sept.	23 July – 22 August
6	Virgo	Kanya	The Virgin	♍	16 Sept. -15 Oct.	23 August – 23 Sept.
7	Libra	Tula	The Balance	♎	16 Oct. -16 Nov.	24 Sept. – 23 Oct.
8	Scorpio	Vrischika	The Scorpion	♏	16 Nov. -15 Dec.	24 Oct. – 22 Nov.
9	Sagittarius	Dhanu	The Archer	♐	16 Dec. -14 Jan.	23 Nov. – 21 Dec.
10	Capricorn	Makar	The Goat	♑	15 Jan. -14 Feb.	22 Dec. – 20 January
11	Aquarius	Kumbh	The Water Bearer	♒	15 Feb. -14 March	21 Jan. – 19 February
12	Pisces	Meen	The Fishes	♓	15 March -14 April	20 Feb. – 20 March

Now the zodiac signs are governed by nine planets, and nine planets are connected to nine numbers. So the zodiacs are also connected to numerology.

ZODIAC NUMEROLOGY CHART

Zodiac Sign	Number	Ruling Planet	Western Time frame	Effect	Qualities
Aries	9	Mars	21 Mar - 20 Apr	Positive	Aggressive, strong passionate, very energetic, powerful, determined, revengeful, unforgiving.
Tauras	6	Venus	21 Apr to 20 May	Positive	Luxury, beauty, entertainment, abundance, art, creativity, love, family, reproduction, travelling, bossy, critical, interfering.
Gemini	5	Mercury	21 May to 20 Jun	Positive	Freedom, Fast moving, versatile, multitalented, adventurous, governs communication, adaptability, addictive, changeable, intolerant.
Cancer	2	Moon	21 June to 20 July	Positive	Emotional, loves water, defines flow, money flow, travel, duality, confusion, related to mind.
Leo	1	Sun	21 July to 20 Aug	Positive	Leader, King, royal, powerful, authority, discipline, egoistic,
Virgo	5	Mercury	21 Aug to 20 Sep	Negative	multitalented, adventurous, governs communication, adaptability, addictive, changeable, intolerant.
Libra	6	Venus	21 Sep to 20 Oct	Negative	Seeking balance is one of the core qualities. Luxury, beauty, entertainment, abundance, art, creativity, love, family, reproduction.
Scorpion	9	Mars	21 Oct to 20 Nov	Negative	Aggressive, strong, passionate, compassionate, intimate in their love affairs, enduring, very energetic, powerful, determined, revengeful, unforgiving.
Sagittarius	3	Jupiter	21 Nov to 20 Dec	Positive	Fun loving, expressive, social, optimistic, humorous, imaginative, creative, friendly, gossipy.
Capricorn	8	Saturn	21 Dec to 20 Jan	Negative	Ambitious, hardworking, struggle, delay, pain, unorganized, strong, driven, wealth conscious.
Aquarius	8	Saturn	21 Jan to 20 Feb	Positive	Ambitious, hardworking, struggle, delay, pain, organized, strong, driven, wealth conscious,
Pisces	3	Jupiter	21 Feb to 20 March	Negative	Fun loving, expressive, social, optimistic, humorous, imaginative, creative, friendly, gossipy.

E.g., if someone is born on the 7th of July, like MS Dhoni, his zodiac sign according to Western astrology is Cancer, and the ruling planet of Cancer is the moon, so his Zodiac number according to Western astrology is 2, which is the number connected to the planet moon of Navagraha.

But if we follow Vedic astrology, then his Zodiac sign is Gemini, and the ruling planet of Gemini is Mercury, and the number connected to Mercury is 5, which becomes his Zodiac number.

The Zodiac number can further help one understand the nature and behaviour pattern of the person.

KARMIC NUMBERS

KARMIC NUMBERS

A concept in numerology that relates to the karmas of past lives.

In our current lives, our souls often carry both wisdom and burdens from past lives, including the mistakes we made.

This clearly explains why some people are gifted with a life of luxury while others are poverty stricken.

In numerology, a karmic number is a specific number that is associated with certain challenges or lessons that an individual may need to address in their current life due to past actions or behaviours.

In numerology, one can observe the impact of karmic numbers in one's life due to their presence in the core numbers like your Root Number, Life path numbers, or name numbers, or personal day, personal month, personal year number, or sun number.

Often, karmic debt numbers are written as the number and then the sum of their numbers—13/4, 14/5, 16/7, and 19/1.

The karmic debt numbers 13, 14, 16, and 19 have a common pattern. The number 1 in each of them signifies selfish misuse of the number that follows. The succeeding number points to the area where this selfishness played out:

- In 13, the number 3 (creativity, energy, and joyfulness) turns into frivolity and superficiality.

- In 14, the number 4 (discipline, hard work, accountability, and stability) transforms into rebelliousness and indulgence as an attempt to escape responsibilities.
- In 16, the number 6 (love and commitment) has been neglected.
- In 19, the number 9 (wisdom, knowledge, and power) has been utilized for personal gain.

The impact and intensity of karmic numbers are dependent on where they appear in one's chart. The strongest impact is on the people born on these dates of any month.

Karmic numbers are also said to be like blessings in disguise. Its presence can be an enlightening lesson that lets you go through turmoil to face any challenges and helps you attain something greater. The best thing is to accept them and be ready to pay the Karmic debts required of them.

MASTER NUMBERS

*I*n numerology, the master numbers are 11, 22, and 33. These numbers are more powerful than other numbers because they are paired together.

The meaning of the master numbers

- 11: The Visionary
- 22: The Planner/ The Builder
- 33: The Messenger

These numbers embody the three stages of creation: visualizing, creating, and sharing.

What makes these numbers unique is that they bring together the qualities of their components, essentially offering a double serving.

For instance, the number 11 combines the power of 1 with the sensitivity of 2, making it confidently intuitive.

Similarly, 22 merges the intuition of 2 with the practicality of 4, earning it the title of Master Builder.

Lastly, 33 blends the creativity of 3 with the compassion and responsibility of 6, making it a highly promising combination.

When found during calculations, Master Numbers are rarely reduced.

For example, Let's look at someone born on November 22, 1983:

- The birthday is 22, which is a Master number.
- November is the 11th month, so there is a Master number 11.

COMPATIBILITY OF NUMBERS/ RELATIONSHIP BETWEEN NUMBERS

I am sure you would agree if I said that you are friendly with some people while you just can't stand others. With some people, you want to be with them for life, and you just want others to get out of your sight. With someone, you might feel like your soulmate, while others might feel like your enemy. Numerology has answers to this compatibility relationship between two people.

In Numerology, each number is said to have a certain type of energy, nature, characteristics, likes, dislikes, choices, tastes, and behaviour patterns. Since each number is associated with a particular planet of the Navagraha that affects and determines life, some numbers are more amicable and harmonious with particular sets of numbers while being hostile toward others. This compatibility is very useful in understanding and determining the future of any relationship, whether it is a romantic relationship or a business partnership.

Each number based on the character and story of the planets has a relationship compatibility chart with nine numbers. There are 81 combinations, but that doesn't stop there. The compatibility is also based on the area of application. There are 5 major areas where this is seen: -

1) Romantic relationship compatibility (relationship between two people).
2) Business partnership compatibility (business relationship between two people).
3) Core number compatibility (relationship between root number and life path number).
4) Name number compatibility.
5) Company name number compatibility.

Each area has a different equation and compatibility ratio between numbers. For example, a person with root number 1 might not be very friendly or in a romantic relationship with root number 8, and if they are together, they might have a lot of differences, but together in core numbers or business partnerships, they can do magic.

A person can use his understanding of the nature or energy of each number to identify the perfect match for him. He can also use this to find the perfect name number, company name, business partner, the right team for the right job, and many more applications.

Numbers can make life simpler, better, happier, more successful, and more abundant.

CAREERS AND NUMEROLOGY

CAREERS AND NUMEROLOGY

With my 15 years of experience in the media, I am fully aware of the highs and lows of working in the industry. Before knowing the impact of numbers on my career and using the power of numbers to choose the right career for me, I kept struggling in the job, struggling for stability, struggling for growth, struggling in the wrong company, and being in the wrong industry.

Each number we know has a certain character, which makes it suitable for certain kinds of industries, job roles, and certain companies. Now, millions are suffering because the energy of their numbers is not aligned with the careers they are in. That is the reason we see certain people working half as hard as you and being twice as successful as you. The reason is that their numbers are aligned with the industry they are in, the company they are in, and the roles they are in.

1. Career Success and Numerology:
   - Success is heightened when one's career aligns with their root number and core values.
   - A well-suited profession minimizes challenges and broadens opportunities.
2. Numerology's Impact on Career:
   - Numerology guides career choices by aligning with individual traits and characteristics.
   - Proper alignment simplifies the professional journey.

Understanding numerology and aligning one's numbers with their career can make anyone successful.

While some people are naturally well-versed in the jobs they do, others have the knack of business and can reach the supreme level. How would you know what you should do- The answer is root and life path number.

Numbers like 1, 5, and 8 are the numbers that can do great in an entrepreneur role.

Numbers like 2 and 7 are good at jobs.

Numbers 3 and 6 can do great as independent or freelance workers (like teachers, designers, and artists).

Numbers 4 and 9 can do both - jobs and business because they are hard workers and practical people.

HEALTH AND NUMEROLOGY

Numbers are different energies, and when these get disturbed for any reason, they have a direct impact on a person's health. One extremely thorough way of predicting and treating a person's health issues is through their numerology chart.

The reasons for the energies of the numbers disturbed could be many. Still, the more dominant ones are:

1) Missing Numbers in the numerology chart.
2) Repetitive numbers in the date of birth (e.g., someone born in the year 1999 has a strong impact of the number 9 and its energy being disturbed because of its repetition 3 times).
3) Overuse of a number in mobile number, car number, etc.

Each number is also connected to a certain body part and can affect a particular organ because of its energy being disturbed. For example, number 8 is connected to legs and bones and could cause issues with them if the energies of number 8 are disturbed.

With the right knowledge and use of numerology, one can also understand the superfoods for each number, the health precautions, and remedies to avoid issues.

One can change lifestyle and eating habits to balance the energies of the disturbed numbers. Numerology can give a deep insight into the problems and can suggest remedies and solutions accordingly.

Colin
James
Grace
Audrey
Angela
Antonio
Doro
Mason
Robert
Fedor
Susan
LIAM
Maddison
Aaron
AlEX
Tomoko
Kylie
Jack
JOSE
Ella
Sean
William
Abigail
Sasha
Helen
Boris
Isaak

NAME NUMBER

When it comes to interpersonal relationships, name numbers play a significant role in establishing them, because the sound effects of your name produce certain vibrations, patterns, and expectations. The first name is more important in close relationships, while the full name is more important for official papers and wherever used. Sometimes it may be advisable to change one's name for better compatibility with the root number and life path number.

In the realm of numerology, every word in our name is assigned a specific number. This numerical representation is crucial because it determines how we are identified by our names. It's essential for these numbers to align with our birth numbers, as our recognition is closely tied to our names.

Adjusting the digits in our name by adding or removing alphabets can create harmony with our birth number, influencing aspects of relationships, family, and health.

Name numerology is the part of numerology that uses numbers to learn about a person's character, destiny, and life journey. The central assumption is that each name has a unique energy associated with it, which is determined by the numerical values assigned to each letter.

The name number is derived from the letters in a person's full name at birth and offers insights into their personality traits, strengths, weaknesses, and life purpose.

To calculate the name number, you assign numerical values to each letter of the alphabet and then add up those values to arrive at a single-digit or master number.

However, it is to be ensured that the total first name number or Total name number is not a karmic number, i.e., 13, 14, 16, or 19.

To find your name number, you can:

1. Give a number to each letter in your name. For example, in Chaldean numerology, each letter gets a number from 1 to 8.
2. Add up these numbers to get one single number.
3. If the number has two digits, add those digits together until you have just one digit.

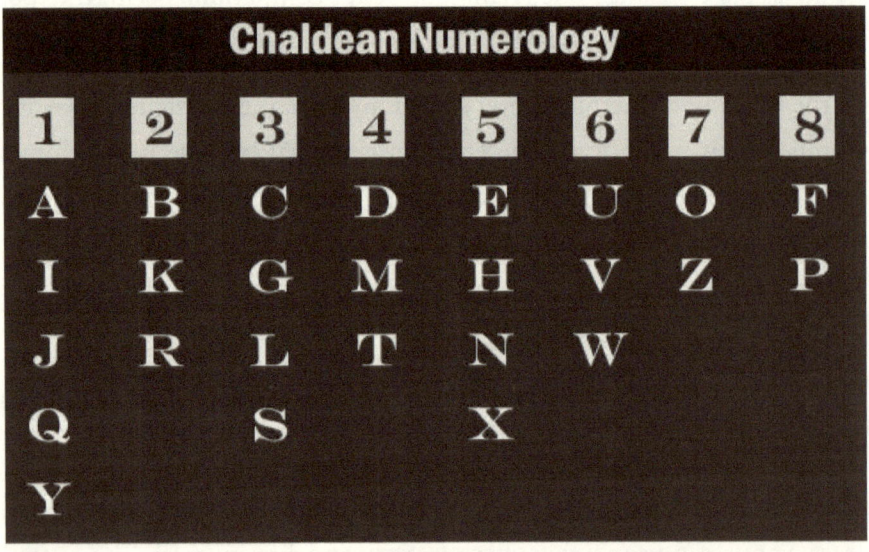

Western countries consider names to be the most important aspect and follow the Pythagorean numerology chart.

Pythagorean Numerology

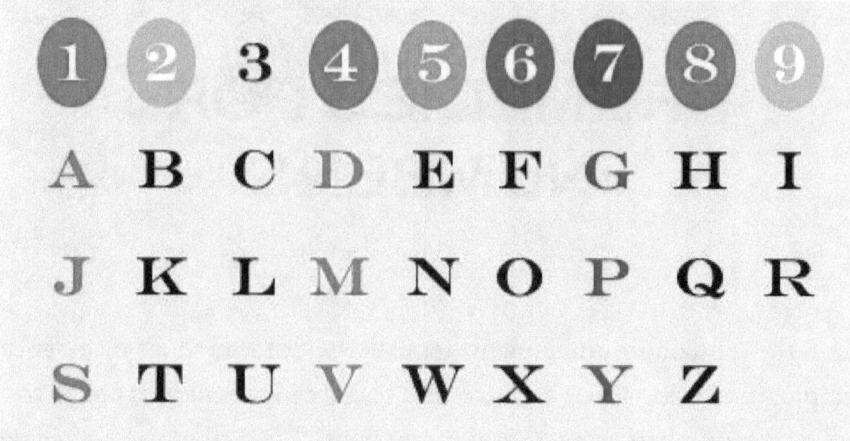

A person's name is a crucial part of who they are—it's their main identity. We often know and identify famous individuals by their names, underlining the significance of names in numerology.

Numerologists also look at the compatibility of an individual's name number, much like they do with birth dates. A name is considered fortunate or excellent for a person if the vibrations associated with the name number match the person's birthdate.

REMEDIES FOR NUMBERS

*I*n the domain of numerology, remedies refer to methods or practices employed to bring about harmony and balance to the energies linked with particular numbers, names, or life situations. The goal of these remedies is to amplify the positive characteristics and alleviate any challenges indicated by numerological factors.

Elemental Remedies

In Feng Shui, each of the nine numbers is associated with one of the five elements—Wood, Fire, Earth, Metal, and Water. The pairing of numbers and elements contributes to the balance and harmony sought in Feng Shui practices. Number 1 corresponds with Water, representing fluidity and the flow of new beginnings. Numbers 2, 5 and 8 align with Earth, emphasizing stability and balance. Numbers 3 and 4 are linked to Wood, signifying growth, expansion, and vitality. Fire is connected with Number 9, symbolizing passion, transformation, and illumination. Metal is attributed to Numbers 6 and 7, embodying strength, precision, and efficiency.

In Feng Shui, the elemental associations of the numbers provide insights into potential remedies to balance energies when certain numbers are disturbed.

By understanding these elemental connections, individuals can use specific remedies to harmonize the energies influenced by their numerological associations in Feng Shui practices.

Yantras

Yantras are geometrical patterns that are designed in such a way that each pattern is connected to a planet and its energy.

The yantras bring in the positive vibrations of those planets and help us overcome the negative effects of those planets in our lives.

Each planet has a specific yantra that can be drawn, printed, or engraved on a metal plate or paper and placed in a suitable direction.

Mantras

- Mantras are sacred sounds or words that have a specific meaning and vibration.
- They are used to invoke the power and blessings of the planets and their deities.
- They should be recited daily to reduce the negative effects of the nine planets in our zodiac signs.
- They should be recited for 40 or 41 days to get best results.
- We need to feel the vibrations of these mantras while reciting them.

Beej Mantras

- Beej mantras are seed sounds that contain the essence of the planets and their energies.
- They are used to pacify or strengthen the planets in our chart, according to both numerology and astrology.
- For each planet, there is a specific Beej mantra that should be recited a certain number of times over a period of time.

Lucky Gemstone

According to numerology, certain energies and vibrations that are claimed to be possessed by gemstones can be utilised as remedies to enhance particular attributes or correct imbalances related to a given number or the planet connected.

LUCKY VEHICLE NUMBER

To calculate the numerological value of the vehicle number, add all the digits of the registration number until you get a single digit number. For example, if the vehicle number is 2345, the numerological value of the vehicle number 2345 is 5. Even the alphabets of the vehicle number are to be added until they get a single digit. The vehicle number should be compatible with the owner's (Registered Name) and also be compatible with the name number.

The choice of a car number should be made with consideration of the following points:

1. Avoid Repetition of Zero:
   - Ensure that the number chosen does not have multiple occurrences of zero.
2. Opt for Ascending Order:
   - Consider selecting numbers in ascending order, such as 14125.
3. Compatibility with Owner's Life Path and Name Numbers:
   - The car number should align with the owner's Life Path Number and Name Number for optimal compatibility.

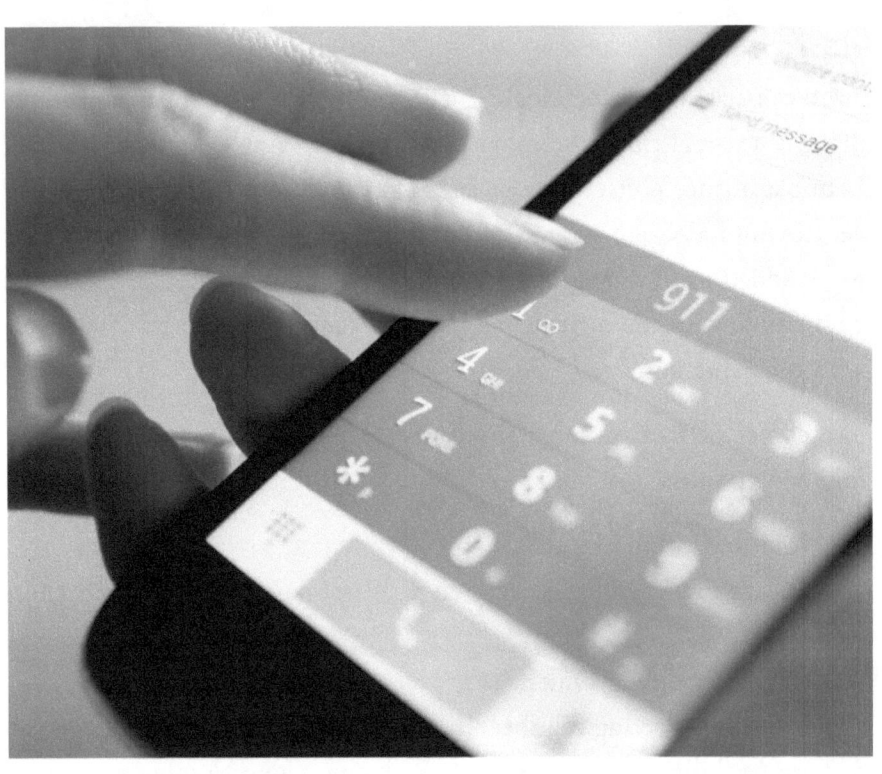

LUCKY MOBILE NUMBER

*I*n this contemporary era, considering the significance of communication and social media platforms, it can be concluded that it is hardly possible for anyone to survive without a mobile. It is important as we do business through mobile, we build relations, we make financial transactions through mobile, and we stay connected with the world with our mobile number.

In numerology, numbers have their own specific vibrations. And the Mobile Number has number vibrations. The mobile number is one that becomes very important as it is directly linked to us and influences our lives. Mobile numbers are being used abundantly daily. The mobile is always with us when we are in a meeting, business deal, interview, job, office, home, etc. Such an important role does the number we carry play.

We need to choose the right mobile number for our careers and relationships.

We should consider the compatibility of the mobile number with our name number and our careers.

Add the digits in your mobile number to a single digit.

For example, If your Mobile Number is 9813000516, then add all the digits and bring the sum down to a single number 9+8+1+3+0+0+0+5+1+6 = 33 = 6.

LUCKY HOUSE NUMBER

*I*t is undeniably true that the only place that makes us feel at ease is our house, and no one can deny the fact that it's the only place that plays a significant role in shaping many aspects of our lives. So house numbers should be favourable to us.

For a rented house, root number compatibility is checked with the house number, whereas for an owned house or property, check the house number compatibility with the life path number. Numbers 13, 14, 16, and 19 are called karmic debt numbers and attract bad news. Hence, it should be avoided.

ACHIEVEMENT
Leadership
STUBBORN
Arrogance
Stubborn
FOCUSED
WILLED
Tunnel Vision
THE PRIMAL FORCE
INDEPENDENT
INDIVIDUALISTIC
CREATIVE
Original
STRONG
ARROGANCE
Individualistic
DRIVE
Stubborn
Ambition
SELFISH
ORIGINAL
INDEPENDENT
Leadership
AMBITION
The Primal Force
FOCUSED
Drive
Focused
Selfish
Leadership
ACHIEVEMENT
STRONG
Ambition
Original
Focused
CREATIVE
INDIVIDUALISTIC
INDEPENDENT

THE NUMBER 1

Root Number 1:

People born on the 1st, 10th, 19th, and 28th of any month are termed as Number 1 people, ruled by the planet Sun. Zodiac Leo is also ruled by the sun.

Birth Number 1:

People born with the birth date of number 1 are linked to the sun, a powerful force known as the soul. So, those with Birth Number 1 are strong and full of energy. They are commanding, make decisions quickly, and are very determined. That's why they often end up being leaders.

When you compel them to do something, they do not consent to do it. They are the best at everything and typically occupy the top spots. They don't mind spending money and take pleasure in life's small pleasures.

Birth Number 10:

The number 10 is a combination of the numbers 1 and 0. If we sum up, it comes to no. 1 again, so it has the qualities of number 1 and zero.

Qualities like newness, possibilities, movement, and independence. The number 1's independent nature helps forge new paths and embrace unexpected possibilities. People born on 10th are also number 1, who like to lead from the front and who perform and work hard to do better in terms of positions.

Birth Number 19:

The number 19 is a combination of the numbers 1 and 9. People with this birth number have qualities of both numbers 1 and 9. Birth number 19 are Pioneering (starting new things), bold, courageous, innovative, self-motivated, determined, independent, leaders, and strong.

Presence of number 9 gives them qualities like empathy, passion, broad-mindedness, compassion, and generosity.

Birth Number 28:

The number 28 combines the numbers 2 and 8. Birth number 28 people have qualities of number 2 like being emotional, people's people, intuitive, and caring.

Whereas presence of number 8 makes them organized, self-motivated, driven, strong, and hardworking.

Famous Celebrities with Root Number 1

Indians Celebrities.

Dhirubhai Ambani: December 28, 1932.

Aishwarya Rai: November 1, 1973.

International Celebrities

Bill Gates October 28, 1955.

Michael Jackson September 1, 1959.

Good Qualities of Numbers 1

The number 1 holds its own unique significance and qualities. Here are some key characteristics associated with the number 1 as per numerology:

1) Leadership: The number 1 is a symbol of leadership, independence, and originality. People with a strong influence of this number tend to be natural leaders who are assertive and confident in their abilities.
2) Initiation: Number 1 represents new beginnings and initiatives. It signifies taking the first step and embarking on a new path. Individuals whose lives are impacted by this number frequently pave new paths and become pioneers and trailblazers.
3) Creativity: This number is linked to creativity and innovation. People associated with the number 1 often have a unique and inventive way of thinking, which helps them stand out in various fields.
4) Influence and Authority: The number 1 is linked to authority and influence. Individuals under its influence may find themselves in positions of power or may have a strong impact on the lives of others.
5) Focus: The number 1 embodies focus and concentration. People with a strong connection to this number are often able to channel their energies into a single goal or project with determination.

Qualities to improve upon for Number 1

1) Flexibility: As natural leaders and initiators, number 1 individuals might sometimes come across as rigid or uncompromising. Developing flexibility and adaptability can help them navigate changing situations and collaborate more effectively with others.
2) Patience: Number 1 personalities tend to be goal-oriented and driven. However, patience might not always be their strong suit. Practising patience can help them avoid rushing into decisions and give them a better perspective on long-term goals.
3) Listening Skills: Being assertive and confident is strength, but it's important for number 1 individuals to also cultivate active listening skills. This will enable them to understand others' perspectives and build stronger relationships.

4) Collaboration: While independence is a strength, collaboration can lead to innovative solutions and a broader support network. Learning to work harmoniously with others can enhance their overall effectiveness.

Ruling Planet and Qualities of Ruling Planet for Number 1

For the number 1, which corresponds to the Sun, Here are some qualities and traits associated with the ruling planet Sun and its influence on the number 1:

1. Leadership: The Sun is associated with leadership qualities. Individuals influenced by the number 1 ruling planet tend to exhibit strong leadership skills and a natural ability to take charge of situations.
2. Independence: The Sun represents independence and self-reliance. People associated with the number 1 ruling planet are often self-confident and prefer to take their own path rather than following the crowd.
3. Creativity: The Sun is linked to creativity and self-expression. The ruling planet of number one tends to inspire creative, inventive thinkers who take pleasure in sharing their gifts and thoughts.
4. Individuality: The Sun emphasises individuality and uniqueness. People with the number 1 ruling planet often stand out due to their distinct qualities and approach to life.
5. Confidence: Confidence is a key attribute of the Sun. People with the number 1 ruling planet tend to possess a high level of self-assurance and self-belief.

Weekday ruled by Number 1

The day ruled by the number 1 is Sunday, which is associated with the planet Sun. Here are some qualities and traits associated with a day ruled by the number 1, i.e., Sunday.

Sunday is traditionally considered the day of the Sun in many cultures. It's often associated with energy, vitality, creativity, and self-expression, which are qualities attributed to the Sun in numerology as well. Many people believe that Sundays are a time to focus on personal growth, leadership, and engaging in activities that bring joy and fulfilment.

Zodiac sign for Number 1

The zodiac sign ruled by Number 1 is Leo, and it has the following qualities and traits:

1. Confident: Leos are known for their inherent confidence and self-assuredness. They often have a strong sense of self and are comfortable in their own skin.
2. Creative: Leo is a creative and expressive sign. Leos tend to possess a natural artistic flair and often excel in creative pursuits.
3. Charismatic: Leos exude a captivating and alluring aura. They are natural leaders in social circumstances because of their contagious excitement and energy, which can attract others.
4. Passionate: Passion runs deep in Leos. They approach life with fervour and are deeply committed to their interests, relationships, and endeavours.
5. Generous: Leos are lavish and enjoy making those around them happy. They have a reputation for being generous and helpful.

Life Path Number 1

If your Life Path Number is 1, it means you're a person who loves setting goals and working hard to achieve them. You're determined and focused on what you want to accomplish in life.

Even in the face of difficulty, you don't give up lightly, and this trait makes you no less of a leader. You're adept at taking charge and making decisions. No challenge can frighten you, and you make extreme efforts to find solutions to problems. In return, you take care of them and show them kindness and respect. But sometimes, if things don't go the way you planned, you might feel frustrated or upset.

Overall, if your life path number is 1, you're someone who works hard to achieve their dreams, cares about others, and has a strong spirit even when things don't go perfectly.

Karmic Number

The karmic number related to Number 1 is Number 19, which is reduced to a single digit that comes to Number 1.

The fundamental idea behind the karmic debt number is that you have some lessons to learn in this lifetime because of the way you treated others in a past life. Karmic debt number 19 is associated with a past-life misuse of power. Individuals with this karmic debt must learn lessons about independence and self-support in the face of life's challenges. It's crucial not to succumb to ego-driven behaviors or stubbornness when dealing with this karmic debt. People with the 19 Karmic Debt will learn the value of independence and responsible use of power. They may find themselves in situations where they have to assert themselves, even if it means standing alone.

Overcoming difficulties through personal struggle is a key aspect of this karmic journey. A central lesson involves recognizing the importance of interdependence, understanding the mutual need for love, and avoiding the self-imposed prison of stubbornly resisting help from others.

Careers for Number 1

Individuals with numerology number 1 are highly focused on their work. They are known for achieving their desires, not only in matters of the heart but also in their professional lives. While they are mindful of their finances, it doesn't necessarily mean they are tight-fisted; rather, they are prudent with their money. Valuing the finer things in life, they also have a knack for securing good deals.

These people are born leaders who use their innovative and driven minds to accomplish their objectives. In terms of numerology career paths, those with number 1 can expect stability and success. They pursue their objectives with tenacity. This holds true for both males and females with the number 1. Women with this number often aspire for independence.

Suitable career options for these individuals include entrepreneurship, law enforcement, top management roles, politics, IAS/IPS, and leading organisational positions.

Compatibility of Number 1 with other Numbers

In numerology, understanding compatibility between different numbers can shed light on how individuals might interact in various contexts, such as core compatibility of planets, relationships, and business partnerships. Here's a brief overview of the compatibility of number 1 with other numbers:

A. Planet Compatibility:

Number 1 represents the planet Sun. Here's a general overview of how planet Sun's qualities might interact with the energies of the other planets represented by numbers 1 to 9:

Sun (1 - Leadership and Self-Expression):
Compatibility: Good.

Moon (2 - Emotions and Nurturing):
Compatibility: Good.

Jupiter (3 - Expansion and Optimism):
Compatibility: Good.

Rahu (4 - Innovation and Practicality):
Compatibility: Not Compatible.

Mercury (5 - Adventure and Change):
Compatibility: Good.

Venus (6 - Harmony and Relationships):
Compatibility: Not Compatible.

Ketu (7 - Intuition and Spirituality):
Compatibility: Not Compatible.

Saturn (8 - Discipline and Structure):
Compatibility: Not Compatible.

Mars (9 - Action and Passion):
Compatibility: Good.

Health for Number 1

It's crucial to keep in mind that numerology provides general insights and should not be used in place of expert medical advice. Here are some health concerns that individuals with Life Path Number 1 might need to pay attention to:

Head-related problems.

Eyes-related problems.

Stomach-related problems.

Heart-related problems.

Lucky Colours for Number 1

For Number 1, which is known for its bold and confident nature, the lucky colours associated with it in numerology are typically light orange and red.

Lucky Numbers for Number 1

Each number is associated with certain numbers that can resonate positively with its energy. For Number 1 individuals,

Most favourable Numbers: 1, 2, 3, 5, and 9.

Most unfavourable Numbers: 4, 6, 7, and 8.

Lucky Days for Number 1

The lucky day for a Number 1 (as per numerology) is Sunday.

Lucky Years for Number 1

One could consider years that align with the number 1 vibration to be fortunate. These years could include those that are numerologically significant for the number 1, such as years that reduce to 1 (e.g., 1, 10, 19, 28).

Years when the Universal Year Number aligns with the energy of the number 1 can also be favourable.

To calculate the Universal Year Number, add the digits of the year. For example, if the year is 2024, the calculation would be 2 + 0 + 2 + 4 = 8. So, 2024 would be a Universal Year 8, and we learned that number 8 is not very compatible with number 1, so people governed by number 1 may face challenges in the year 2024.

A personal year number for you that aligns with the energy of the number 1 can also be favourable.

To calculate the personal year number, add the digits of your Birth date and Birth Month to the current year.

For example, if you were born on April 28 and the current year is 2024, the calculation would be:

2+ 8+ 4 + 2 + 0 + 2 + 4 = 22. 2+2= 4. So, for 2024, your Personal Year Number would be 4.

Universal year that sums up to 1, 2, 3, 5 or 9 would be considered fortunate for numerology number 1 individuals.

So the next 5 lucky years will be,

2025, 2026, 2027, 2028, 2030.

Lucky Name Number for Number 1

A name number that aligns with the vibration of the number 1 may be considered fortunate. This includes names that are numerologically significant for the number 1, such as a name number that adds up to 1, 3, 5, or 9, which is deemed most favourable.

Remedies for Number 1

a) Elemental Remedies

To address missing number 1 in your birthdate, you can consider incorporating elemental remedies that align with the qualities associated with the number 1.

For Missing Number 1:

When the number 1 is absent from your name or birthdate, it could suggest a potential absence of qualities such as being pioneering, bold, courageous, innovative, self-motivated, determined, independent, possessing leadership skills, and being strong.

To address this, you can use the element associated with the number 1, which is water.

- Drink more water and offer water to the sun.

For Repeating Number 1:

If the number 1 is repeated in your name or birthdate, it could bring both positive and challenging aspects into your life.

Here's how you can harness the energy of repeating number 1:

1) Donate Wheat, Jaggery, and red clothes on Sunday.
2) Put a Copper Coin in Running Water.
3) Avoid Wearing Red and Orange Clothes.
4) Offer Water to the Sun.

b) Planet Remedies

Planets are associated with specific numbers and vibrational energies. You can bring Sun Yantra to your home/Office for Number 1.

c) Mantra Remedies

To get the grace of Sun, one should worship the Lord SUN and chant the mantra: "Om Suryay Namah" every day or at least every Sunday 108 times.

d) Beej Mantra Remedies

Similarly, you can harmonize your energy with the attributes of the Sun by chanting Beej mantras associated with it. You can chant the Beej

Mantra "Om Hring Hraung Suryay Namah" every day or at least every Sunday 108 times.

e) Lucky Gemstone

Ruby (a red colour stone) is associated with the Sun.

Bonus Section
a) Lucky Mobile Number

Ensure that the total of all the digits of your mobile number is compatible with the energy of Numbers compatible with Number 1, i.e., 1, 2, 3, 5, 9.

However, make sure that it's not a karmic number, doesn't have any number repeating more than twice, and does not end in Zero.

b) Lucky House Number

Selecting a lucky house number requires taking into account the number's vibrational frequency and how well it matches your intentions and energies. If it's a rented property, make sure that its number is compatible with your root number, and if it's an owned property, its number is compatible with your life path number.

For individuals with Numerology Number 1, certain house numbers might resonate well.

House numbers might be considered lucky for Number 1 individuals: house Numbers adding to 1, 2, 3, 5, or 9.

Avoid house numbers with karmic numbers 13, 14, 16, and 19.

c) Lucky Vehicle Number

Choosing a lucky vehicle number for individuals with number 1 involves considering the energetic qualities of the number and how they align with the individual's energy and intentions.

Those who have Date of Birth 1 or name number 1 should select the vehicle number, adding to either 1, 2, 3, 5, or 9.

SYNOPSIS.

So overall, the number 1 is associated with the planet Sun and the zodiac sign Leo. It's also called the King of Planets. People with number 1 are pioneering, bold, courageous, innovative, self-motivated, determined, independent, leaders, and strong.

Co- Authored by Mr. Sukhminder Singh

COOPERATIVE
DISCONTENT
Oversensitive
SENSUAL
INTUITIVE
WARM
STUDIOUS
Sensitive
Peacemakers
Dependant
SENSUAL
DIPLOMATIC
DEPENDANT
Empathetic
PATIENT
Cooperative
TACTFUL
WARM
LOVING
EMPATHETIC
Studious
Sensitive
TACTFUL
INTUITIVE
PEACEMAKERS
Tactful
Sensual
PEACEMAKERS
Oversensitive
loving
SENSITIVE
The All Knowing
DIPLOMATIC
PATIENT

THE NUMBER 2

Root Number 2

People who are born on the 2nd, 11th, 20th, or 29th of any given month are said to be numerology number 2. Number 2 is governed by the moon, or rather, the moon is the ruling planet. It is also known as a watery planet. The moon is also called the queen of Navagraha.

In numerology, each number holds its own unique significance. When looking at the number 2 as a standalone entity, it embodies 100% of the qualities associated with that number.

However, in the case of 11, it is derived from 1+1, essentially connecting it to the qualities of the number 2 but also having strong qualities of number 1.

2+0= 2,

2+9= 11/ 1+1=2

In this scenario, the total number of 2 is derived from two distinct numbers, creating a compound number. These two separate numbers correspond to different planets, combining to form a single-digit number, specifically, the number 2.

2. Famous Celebrities with Number 2

Let's see the example of some celebrities who come under root number 2.

Have a look at the **Indian celebrities**

1) Shah Rukh Khan – November 2, 1965
2) Rajesh Khanna – December 29, 1942
3) Amitabh Bachchan – October 11, 1942
4) Milkha Singh – November 20, 1929

Some **International Celebrities**

1) Lucas Black – November 29, 1982
2) Leonardo DiCaprio – November 11, 1974
3) Demi Moore – November 11, 1962
4) David Schwimmer – November 2, 1966

Good Qualities of Number 2

Numerology Number 2 Traits:

1. Harmonious, intuitive, caring, and supportive nature.
2. Excellent in diplomacy with a natural understanding of others.
3. Expressive, affectionate, and possessing a strong imagination.
4. Key qualities: Patience, self-confidence, peace-making abilities, and family focus.

Roles and Settings:

1. Instinctively take on helping and guiding roles in various settings.
2. Commonly found in organizations, schools, and colleges.

Leadership and Mediation:

1. Good leaders and adept mediators with skill in handling people.

Qualities to improve upon for Number 2

Their hypersensitivity frequently works against them, and their moodiness leads to boredom, prompting a desire for change. Feelings of jealousy, indecision, and a lack of will to take action are common traits. They panic when confronted with stuck situations because they live in their own world. Individuals with number 2 possess what it takes to be achievers, but like shells under the ocean, they need someone to acknowledge their ability and worthiness and bring out the best in them.

Indecisive: Number 2 always finds a solution, but to find the middle ground between the problems, they often get confused as they want to be unbiased. Therefore, when it comes to making a large or small decision, it becomes difficult.

Hyper Sensitive: They are very sensitive and peaceful and are known for drawing harmony. But the problem occurs because of their sensitivity. This sensitive nature can often lead to hurting themselves badly, which can be very painful.

Unassertive: They constantly compromise their personal comfort and preferences in their haste to bring about tranquilly. If they continue doing it for a long time, there can be an issue. As remaining stagnant at this stage could hurt their mental state, it will be harmful to their health.

Moody: They have frequent mood swings; due to this, they always work as per their emotions and mood, so such people can easily go into depression.

Ruling Planet and Qualities of Ruling Planet for Number

Moon's Position in Navagraha:

- Holds the second spot after the Sun, referred to as the queen.
- Governs emotions, mood, and mental/emotional power.
- Lunar Phases:

- Beautiful round body with 16 kalas, reflecting waxing and waning periods.
- Exhibits two phases: Shukla Paksha (positive) and Krishna Paksha (negative).
- Sweet speech but a fickle mind leading to mood changes.

Influence of Moon:

1. The moon's watery influence brings a natural emotional and lovable demeanor.
2. Exhibits high adaptability and flexibility.
3. Comfortable working behind the scenes, guiding, helping, and displaying generosity.
4. Gentle in nature, easily hurt, but possesses a forgiving disposition.

Characteristics:

1. Gentleness, imagination, artistic tendencies, and a romantic inclination.
2. Strong intuition is linked to mind and emotions, contributing to occasional moodiness.
3. Represents duality, reflecting the planet's association with motherhood and queenship.

Weekday ruled by Number 2

Each planet from 1 to 9 holds unique significance and influences its designated day. The Moon, for instance, is associated with Monday.

The Zodiac ruled by Number 2

The moon governs the zodiac sign Cancer, which represents those born between June 21st and July 20th. Individuals under this sign are known for their attractiveness, moodiness, and possessiveness. Cancers are characterized by their passion, creativity, secrecy, intuition, and caring nature.

As the ruling planet of this number is the moon, which shines by the reflection light of the sun, people of this number are likely to get easily influenced by others. They achieve success under the guidance of their patrons and mentors. They tend to be emotional about certain things in life. Their emotions at times sway them away. The natives of this number show conflict, weakness, and hesitancy.

Life Path Number 2

People who identify with life path number 2 are fundamentally peacemakers who value harmony over hatred. They are exceptional at figuring out balanced solutions to problems. This group is characterized by their sensitivity, emotional depth, strong creativity, diplomatic skills, and a natural aptitude for mediation.

E.g., Jennifer Lopez, (born July 24, 1969, Bronx, New York, U.S.),

Her Life Path number- $2+4+7+1+9+6+9=38$, $3+8=11$, $1+1=2$.

Jennifer Lopez is renowned for her versatility, excelling as a singer, dancer, actress, and producer. She has set a benchmark and remains one of the idols worth looking up to for her formidable talent. While she exhibits weaknesses in indecision and extreme sensitivity, Jennifer Lopez is celebrated for her impeccable fashion sense, setting trends, and influencing the style world. Throughout her career, she has shown immense perseverance and determination to overcome obstacles and achieve success.

Actively engaged in charitable activities and humanitarian causes, her dedication to achieving excellence may create tensions in certain professional domains. Jennifer Lopez embodies the qualities linked with the numerological number 2, which stands for marriage and relationships, having been married multiple times and having children.

Another example of an Indian celebrity

Name: Aamir Khan

Date of Birth: March 14, 1965.

Life Path Number: 1+4+3+1+9+6+5= 29/2.

As a life path number 2 person, prominent Indian actor, producer, and director Aamir Khan personifies the traits of a diplomat and a peacemaker. Known as the "Perfectionist" of Bollywood, he is celebrated for his meticulous approach to acting and commitment to socially relevant cinema. Life Path number 2 individuals, like Aamir Khan, are gentle, caring, and collaborative. Khan demonstrates this through his engagement in social causes, utilizing his platform to raise awareness. While celebrated for versatility and a clean image, his overly critical and moody nature aligns with traits associated with number 2.

Master Number 11

11: Visionary, idealistic, teacher, sensitive, a perfectionist, aloof.

For individuals born on the 11th of any given month, this unique number holds significance. 11 is recognized as a master number, symbolizing leadership, initiative, confidence, communication, the soul, and intuition.

The equation 1+1=2 emphasizes the duality inherent in this number, showcasing dual qualities. Often referred to as the Master Intuitive number, those born on the 11th are encouraged to engage in creative pursuits. The amalgamation of the 2 in the date strengthens the impact of these masterful and intuitive qualities.

The number 11 is super intuitive. It brings illumination and connects with our inner feelings without needing logical thinking. It's linked to sensitivity, nervous energy, shyness, and dreaming big. The 11 has everything that the number 2 has, but with extra charisma, leadership, and inspiration.

Careers for Number

As we are talking about the people born on 2/11/20 and 29 of any month, number 2 is a number of duality /co-operation/peacemaker.

Individuals with numerology number 2 are adept at communication and excel in interpersonal relationships, making them successful in both jobs and businesses.

People with number 2 are mostly known for their emotional complexity and inventiveness, and they are successful in creative industries like music, dance, print, and art. Their outstanding communication abilities also put them in a good position in fields like nursing, teaching, human resources, and medicine.

In the business realm, individuals with the number 2 flourish, particularly in liquid businesses. Ventures involving white products like milk, sweets, paneer, sugar, and rice align well with their capabilities. Additionally, they excel in overseas ventures and travel-related enterprises.

Top Recommended Career Paths:

1. Liquid Business/Food
2. Management
3. Public Relations/Human Resources.

Compatibility of Number 2 with other Numbers

Number 2 displays varying degrees of compatibility with other numbers:

1. No. 2 is compatible with No. 1:
   - Harmony exists in this pairing.
2. No. 2 is compatible with No. 2:
   - Similarities lead to compatibility in this match.

3. No. 2 is compatible with No. 3:
   - Knowledge and emotion combine to form a potentially powerful combination that makes for a good couple.
4. No. 2 with No. 4:
   - While planet wise they may not align perfectly, No. 4's reliability and hardworking nature can complement No. 2.
5. No. 2 with No. 5:
   - Not an ideal combination due to planetary differences, as Moon (No.2) and Mercury (No.5) have conflicting personalities.
6. No. 2 with No.6:
   - Quality-wise, they function well in relationships, but planetary influences (Daitya Guru) may pose challenges.
7. No. 2 with No.7:
   - Negative compatibility both planet-wise and in terms of qualities, as the eclipse-creating nature of 7 (Ketu) clashes with No. 2.
8. No. 2 with No. 8:
   - Energy-wise compatibility exists, but there are differences in nature and only average compatibility in relationships.
9. No. 2 with No. 9:
   - Despite having different personalities and being on opposite planets, there is still a strong attraction in relationships. These compatibility assessments provide insights into how number 2 interacts with other numbers.

Health for Number 2

The moon denotes mind /emotions. If your mind gets disturbed, then it will affect the body-related problem, and 70% of our body is made with Water. Ensure intake of lots of water, as it is directly connected to the Moon.

The moon can cause depression. Insomnia, asthma, and blood-related problems.

Lucky Colours for Number 2

Number 2 is governed by the moon and its color is white. Since number 2 is compatible with most numbers, it can also wear other colors, except red and black.

Lucky Numbers for Number 2

1 and 2 are lucky numbers for number 2 individuals. Numbers 3 and 6 are neutral to the number 2.

Lucky Days for Number 2

Mondays and Sundays, but on Mondays, do not start anything new.

Lucky Years for Number 2

Lucky years are 2026, 2027, 2028, and 2031.

Luck Name Number for Number 2

According to numerology, it is not great if a first name and a full name come on number 2. They might in life due to a lack of consistency and mood changes.

The significance of one's name number is crucial in an individual's life. For optimal results, the first name should avoid coming at 2, 4, 7, and 8, and should not combine with karmic numbers like 13, 14, 16, and 19.

Number 2 can bring their name number to compatible numbers like 1, 3, or 6.

Remedies for Number 2

In numerology, missing or repeating numbers in your name or birthdate can indicate certain energy imbalances or strengths.

Elemental Remedies

To address the missing number 2 in your name or birthdate, you can consider incorporating remedies that align with the element associated with the number 2.

Number 2 people should wear items made from Earth.

Wear a clear quartz crystal bracelet or necklace.

For Repeating Number 2

When the number 2 appears more than twice in an individual's chart, certain remedies can be followed to balance its influence.

Donate white items on Monday:

- Offer donations of white items such as barfi, milk, rice, kheer, white clothes, silver, sugar, curd, white flowers, etc. on Mondays.

a) Planet Remedies

Planets are associated with specific numbers and vibrational energies.

Have Darshan of Lord Shiv, especially on Monday, offer water or milk.

The moon signifies mother, so take one silver coin from her as a blessing and always keep it with you.

b) Mantra Remedies

Chant 108-times

Om Chandray Namah or Om Somay Namah on Mondays.

c) Beej Mantra Remedies

Should do Chanting of Mantra 108 times

"Om Aing Kling Somay Namah" on Mondays or

Aum Shram Shrim Shrom Seh Chandraye Namah.

d) Lucky Gemstone (Only Post Astrologer Recommendation)

According to numerology, certain energies and vibrations that are thought to be carried by gemstones can be used as remedies to enhance particular qualities or correct imbalances related to a given number or planet.

A pearl is a gemstone for the moon, as it denotes water, and pearls are found inside the water, which is controlled by the moon.

Gemstones have a very strong effect, and that's why we should wear gemstones only after a recommendation by an Astrologer.

1. Bonus Section
a) Lucky Mobile Number

We should always choose a mobile number that is compatible with your root number. In this case, ensure that the total of all your digits in your mobile number is compatible with the energy of numbers compatible with number 2.

The mobile number 2 is the perfect number for people who love art and music and are romantic. It depicts emotions, care, and a fluctuating mind.

However, make sure that it's not a Karmic Number, doesn't have any number repeating more than twice, and does not end in zero.

Number 2 people can have a total mobile number, adding to numbers 1, 2, 3, or 6.

b) Lucky House Number

House numbers are also very important for us. So while choosing a house we should ensure that the house number is compatible with your root numbers & with life path numbers, and the house number should not come to karmic numbers like 13, 14, 16, & 19.

House Number 2:

When the total of a house number adds up to 2, it signifies qualities of quiet energy, a cooperative environment, companionship, and sentimentality. Despite these positive attributes, there are certain challenges associated with house number 2.

Challenges for Independent Individuals:

- It may pose difficulties for those who value independence highly.

A tendency towards Sensitivity:
- The energy of Number 2 can lead to heightened sensitivity in the household.

c) Lucky Vehicle Number

Number 2 people should drive car numbers totaling 1, 3, or 6. Car number 2 may make you travel a lot.

Synopsis:

The number 2 is associated with the captivating beauty of the moon, which completes its cycle in 28 days and undergoes phase changes every 14 days. Number 2 is inherently intuitive, pleasant, emotional, and extremely sensitive by nature, reflecting its association with the mind of the body.

Co-Authored by: AmolOmBaldi and Ashmitta Vishwakarrma

THE NUMBER 3

THE NUMBER 3

Root Number 3

Individuals born on the 3rd, 12th, 21st, or 30th of any month are ruled by numerology number 3, which is connected to the planet Jupiter of the Navagraha.

Famous celebrities

Rajinikanth (12/Dec),
Swami Vivekananda (12/Jan),
Rani Mukerji (21/Mar),
Vivek Anand Oberoi (3/Sep),
Kareena Kapoor (21/Sep),
Yuvraj Singh (12/Dec),
Abraham Lincoln (12/Feb),
Warren Buffett (30/Aug).

Good Qualities of Number 3

In the world of numbers, 3 is all about spirituality and strong feelings, blending the qualities of one and two. People who are under the influence of number 3 are naturally optimistic, and no hurdle can put an end to their zeal because of their good sense of humour and creativity. They're charming, loyal, and trustworthy.

Number 3 individuals are emotional, sanguine, and creative beings. Imagine how cheerful and engaging a family will be when a naughty kid commits playful atrocities. Then an individual with the number 3 is the epitome of liveliness. Number 3 is gifted with creativity and inspires the people around him/her. This number is always cheerful, optimistic, and full of enthusiasm, kind of like the sunshine number that brings positive vibes. It's all over the place, spreading its energy outward, and is the happy-go-lucky member of the number crew.

Qualities to improve upon for Number 3

They're usually friendly and smart, but sometimes they can be a bit dramatic and love attention. On the downside, they might enjoy gossip, be a bit rude , or show signs of being too proud at times. It's like they have different sides to their personalities. They can also be overly critical, picky, and nagging, especially in women.

Other not-so-great traits include being self-righteous, cruel, dictatorial, hypocritical, spending too much, having a big ego, being vain, having false pride, and boasting a lot.

Ruling Planet and Qualities of Ruling Planet for Number 3

In numerology, the number 3 is quite special, connected with the revered teacher of the Gods, Dev Guru Brihaspati. Those with the Root number 3 individuals, influenced by Jupiter, embody intelligence, sociability, and generosity. While this influence contributes to career success, it may strain relationships and induce stress due to a need for strict discipline. Jupiter, the ruling planet of Number 3, is associated with wisdom and knowledge. Thursday is considered the lucky day for those influenced by Jupiter in numerology.

Jupiter's Qualities:

1. Wisdom and Knowledge: Linked to wisdom and love for learning.

2. Abundance and Expansion: Encourages growth and exploration of opportunities.
3. Generosity and Benevolence: Associated with a charitable and compassionate nature.
4. Optimism and Enthusiasm: Characterized by positivity and an enthusiastic approach to challenges.
5. Spirituality: Strong ties to spiritual exploration and higher knowledge.
6. Leadership and Authority: Instills qualities of leadership and authority.
7. Luck and Fortune: Traditionally associated with good luck and positive outcomes.

Root number 3 individuals are skilled communicators but may struggle with execution due to impatience. Despite initial challenges, they shine, experiencing inner growth. Considered "scientists of life," they are confident decision-makers with strong intellect, stamina, and versatility contributing to their success.

Weekday ruled by Number 3

Jupiter, the largest planet in our solar system, holds a prominent place in astrology and is associated with a myriad of qualities. In numerology, Thursday is considered the lucky day for individuals influenced by the planet Jupiter.

Since Thursday is associated with Jupiter, it is considered a lucky day for those with root number 3. Good vibes envelop them on this special day.

If you're a Root number 3, consider making important decisions or planning significant events on Thursdays.

Zodiac signs for Number 3

People born between November 21st and December 20th fall under the zodiac sign Sagittarius, while those born between February 21st and March 20th belong to Pisces.

In the realm of numerology, these individuals are connected with the number 3, as the ruling planet of both zodiacs is Jupiter, and Jupiter is connected to the Number 3, which brings both special qualities and challenges to their lives.

For those affected by the energy of number 3, striking a harmonious balance between remaining disciplined and gregarious is essential. This balance ensures a positive and fulfilling life journey for individuals guided by the characteristics of Sagittarius and Pisces in connection with the number 3.

Life Path Number 3

In the world of numerology, the number "Three" is like the life of the party–always lively and entertaining. These individuals are creative, outgoing, and love being in the limelight, even if they don't actively seek it. Threes enjoy expressing themselves in various ways, from their fashion choices to how they communicate. Many 3s are drawn to the arts and entertainment, either as a passion or a profession. However, their love for making everything a bit theatrical can make them a bit dramatic. The best side of the Threes shines with optimism, generosity, and charisma, while their less favourable traits can include being directionless, superficial, and moody. Overall, the Threes embrace life with enthusiasm and vibrancy.

Example- Rajinikanth, the superstar of India, has life path no. 3, His DOB is 12-12-1950 (1+2+1+2+1+9+5=21/2+1=3).

If you calculate your life path number and find you're on life path 3, it means you have leadership qualities and are driven by your imagination.

Threes can express their artistic energy, are highly creative, and have excellent communication skills. They also have a great deal of knowledge and optimism.

Careers for Number 3

People with a life path number of 3 are super creative and thrive in careers where they can explore new and exciting ideas. Besides the obvious choices like performing arts, they might also enjoy careers such as fashion design, photography, or writing.

It may be a sign that it's time to showcase your abilities to the world if you consistently see the number 3 everywhere you look. Seek opportunities to hone your abilities, expand your knowledge, and establish a connection with your higher purpose. It's like a nudge from the universe to let your creativity shine and make a positive impact.

Number 3 is entertaining, creative, and imaginative. They always work to uplift their future. They are extremely good in the entertainment and creative industries. They are good at expressing their art.

People with number 3 are fantastic artists, actors, entertainers, writers, speakers, teachers, guides, counsellors, philosophers, writers, professors, salespeople, interior designers, therapists, chefs, and hair, make-up and clothing stylists.

Compatibility of Number 3 with other Numbers

Being in a relationship with number 3 is quite exciting. If you're a 3, you love having a good time, and relationships with you are never dull because you're always adding some excitement to keep things interesting, especially in the bedroom. While you find joy in the fun side of intimacy, true closeness might be a bit challenging. The reason is that deep down, a 3 may struggle with feelings of insecurity and a fear of being seen as empty inside.

In tough times, a 3 might turn to self-pity or substance use. However, with the support of a caring friend, partner, or mentor, a 3 can overcome these challenges by facing fears and building a solid foundation for their naturally happy personality.

The compatibility of numerology number 3 with all 9 numbers:

1. Compatibility of number 3 with Number 1:
   - Harmonious partnership, but potential for conflict due to the 1's critical nature.
2. Compatibility of number 3 with Number 2:
   - Generally compatible, but differences in communication styles may require patience.
3. Compatibility of number 3 with Number 3:
   - Good understanding and compatibility, sharing similar traits and energy.
4. Compatibility of number 3 with Number 4:
   - Neutral relationship, neither particularly good nor bad, requiring compromise.
5. Compatibility of number 3 with Number 5:
   - Exciting and adventurous partnership, but may need the effort to establish stability.
6. Compatibility of number 3 with Number 6:
   - Complementary energies number wise but contradict planet wise(Jupiter and Venus). Have the potential for a balanced and harmonious relationship or firecrackers.
7. Compatibility of number 3 with Number 7:
   - Differences in approach to life may lead to challenges, but there is potential for growth.
8. Compatibility of number 3 with Number 8:
   - Strong potential for success and achievement when combining energies.
9. Compatibility of number 3 with Number 9:
   - Generally compatible, with shared ideals and the potential for a meaningful connection.

Health for Number 3

People born on the 3rd, 12th, 21st, and 30th of any month are influenced by the planet Jupiter. This planet's impact on their health is notable, as it governs organs like the liver, lungs, and veins. Individuals with this influence may face health challenges such as chest or lung disorders, skin problems, diabetes, sore throats, and arthritis.

They ought to exercise caution to avoid overstressing their nervous system. Adopting a diet that avoids fatty meals and includes fruits like apples, pomegranates, grapes, pineapples, and cherries, along with almonds and cloves, is recommended for their well-being.

Although generally robust, number 3 individuals should be mindful of their vulnerabilities to conditions like asthma, allergies, and skin issues. It's essential to balance their disciplined lifestyle with caution against excessive partying and unhealthy habits.

Lucky Colours for Number 3

In numerology, each number is linked to specific planets, and the association between the colour yellow and the number 3 stems from the influence of Jupiter, the ruling planet of number 3.

Jupiter is often associated with expansive qualities, wisdom, and positivity. Due to its association with Jupiter's energy, yellow is auspicious for those under the influence of number 3.

Yellow symbolizes brightness, optimism, and vibrant energy that resonates well with the characteristics of the number 3. Wearing yellow or incorporating it into one's surroundings is believed to enhance the positive attributes associated with Jupiter's influence.

Those whose lives are governed by the energy of the number 3 and Jupiter are believed to benefit from this colour in terms of prosperity, good fortune, and overall well-being.

Lucky Numbers for Number 3

The designation of 3, 1, and 9 as lucky numbers for numerology number 3 is rooted in the belief that certain numbers carry specific vibrations or energies that align harmoniously with individuals influenced by number 3.

Lucky Days for Number 3

Thursday, identified as the auspicious day for individuals with number 3 in numerology, is considered significant due to its association with the planet Jupiter. Even Sundays and Tuesdays are good days for number 3.

Lucky Years for Number 3

Individuals linked to numerology number 3 can identify their lucky years by recognizing the cyclical nature of numerology and observing repeating patterns over time. According to the concept of universal years, the favourable years for number 3 natives are those adding up to 1, 3, 5, and 9. This includes years like 2025, 2026, and 2028.

Lucky Name Number for Number 3

Name numbers added to 1, 2, 3, 5, 7, 8, and 9 are considered friendly to number 3.

In numerology, if the name number matches these friendly numbers and the sum of the first or full name is 3, it suggests that the person possesses qualities like intelligence, ambition, sociability, and a good personality.

Individuals associated with the number 3 may seek remedies to enhance their energy. One approach is to ensure that the name numbers align harmoniously with the friendly numbers of 3.

By doing so, individuals can enhance the positive attributes associated with their root number 3, promoting qualities such as intelligence, ambition, and sociability.

Remedies for Number 3

a) Elemental Remedies/Missing Number 3 Remedies

Balancing Number 3 Energy

If your chart lacks the influence of number 3, there are simple remedies to reintroduce its positive energy.

You can wear a wooden bracelet, use a tulsi rosary, or keep any wooden object close to you. These items are believed to bring the energy of the wood element into your life, helping to restore balance.

In numerology, these remedies are seen as a way to connect with specific energies associated with numbers, promoting a sense of completeness and well-being.

Remedies for Repeated numbers 3

Donate yellow things like bananas, mangoes, gram dal, turmeric, yellow cloth, jaggery, yellow flowers, etc. on Thursday.

Avoid wearing yellow clothes.

Planet Remedies

To receive the blessings of the divine teacher, Devguru Jupiter, individuals can contribute items such as topaz, saffron, gram lentils, turmeric, and yellow clothes to a deserving Brahmin in the morning, based on their capacity.

Mantra Remedies

Mantra Remedy: Chanting mantras is like a positive practice to tap into the good vibes of Jupiter for number 3.

For number 3, the mantra is "Om Brihaspataye Namah" or "Om guruve namah." It's even better if you wear something yellow while doing it. Just recite this mantra 108 times every day or on Thursdays.

Beej Mantra Remedies

Beej Mantras are like super-powered mantras, and each planet has its special one. To boost the good vibes of number 3, you should chant the Beej Mantra of Jupiter, and chanting 108 times helps you get more connected to the planet's energy.

Jupiter Beej Mantra "Hring Kleeng hung Brihasptye Namah."

Lucky Gemstone

Different gemstones have different metal rings, and you need to know the right way to wear them. For number 3, connected to Jupiter, the gemstone is yellow sapphire.

Although gemstones are unique stones, it's advisable to seek guidance from a qualified astrologer before wearing one.

Bonus Section

a) Lucky Mobile Number

Mobile Number: If the total of all the digits in your mobile number adds up to 3, it's considered good for family matters. Numbers like 2, 3, and 6 are excellent for personal use, and numbers 1 and 9 are for professional use.

b) Lucky House Number

House Number: If your house has the number 3, associated with Jupiter, it signifies family, laughter, and entertainment. But occasionally, it can result in family members getting worked up and criticizing each other's deeds, which will ultimately create a bitter atmosphere. More people frequently stay at this house.

Lucky Vehicle Number

Car Number: In today's world, everyone owns a car, and the numbers on that car can impact our lives. Knowing the car number and the right colour for the car is essential. For family and health, number 3 is considered good for the vehicle.

It's advisable to avoid car numbers 4, 7, and 8.

Synopsis

Numerology number 3 is all about intelligence, sociability, and generosity, influenced by the planet Jupiter. People with this number are positive thinkers, often charming, loyal, and trustworthy. The planet Jupiter, associated with wisdom, makes Thursday the lucky day for number 3 individuals. Known for their excellent communication skills, they can be outspoken in public, though impatience may hinder execution.

Despite their early struggles, they shine, becoming versatile and confident decision-makers. Linked to spirituality and leadership, number 3 is considered fortunate in years adding up to 1, 3, 5, and 9, such as 2025 and 2028.

Co-Authored by Rittuu Ajjay Gupta and Amita Bishnoi

THE NUMBER 4

THE NUMBER 4

Root Number 4

We now know that the root number is the sum of the digits of your birthday, irrespective of any month. So, all the people who are born on the 4th, 13th, 22nd, or 31st of any month have root number 4, and they are governed by the planet Rahu. All the people having root number 4 will have some similarities, but of course, they are all different from each other.

Birth Number 4

A person born on the 4th of any month is a pure number 4 and is likely to have most of the qualities of the number 4, which is governed by the planet Rahu. Such people are disciplined, hard-working, and organized. They love to do everything in a systematic process and execute everything in a well-planned way. They have a focused and practical approach to life; they are aspirational, goal-oriented individuals who are prepared to endure the hardships necessary to reach their objectives. The fourth group consists of highly intelligent and perceptive individuals whose knowledge and self-assurance can make them excellent leaders.

Number 4 people have a very strong persona; they are stable-minded, reliable, and always grounded. They don't get scared of challenges easily but rather overcome them with confidence.

Birth Number 13

Number 13: A Unique Blend of Traits

The number 13 is unique as it is a strong and influential number. At the same time, it is frequently regarded as unlucky in different cultures. People born on the thirteenth have a special set of traits that are influenced by the numbers 4, 1, and 3. Approximately 50% of their traits align with number 4, while 30% and 20% are derived from numbers 1 and 3, respectively.

These individuals showcase a versatile personality, embodying qualities such as sharp-mindedness, intelligence, focus, and reliability akin to number 4. Additionally, they exhibit traits of humour, sociability, and creativity, like number 3. Their charming and confident demeanor enables them to attract others effortlessly. However, the mix also introduces challenges such as stubbornness, impatience, and egoism.

Karmic Debt of Number 13: A Journey of Redemption

Number 13 carries the weight of karmic debt, suggesting past-life misdeeds that need rectification. This karmic debt is considered the strongest, indicating a haunting past life where the individual misused the positive attributes of number 3, governed by Jupiter.

The karmic debt number 13 is linked to past wrongdoing related to moral values for personal gain, particularly in the realm of work. This debt implies that you'll need to put in extra effort and learn more lessons to achieve success in your career. Individuals with this number may encounter repeated obstacles in reaching their goals but can overcome them by avoiding shortcuts and adopting a more grounded and systematic approach.

Those with a 13 Karmic Debt are hard workers who face challenges repeatedly. They might feel burdened and frustrated by the perceived futility of their efforts, leading them to give up on goals they believe to be unattainable. Some may succumb to laziness and negativity, but success is attainable through hard work and perseverance. Many highly successful individuals in various fields, such as business, art, and sports, carry a 13 Karmic Debt.

Birth Number 22/ Master Number

Understanding individuals born on the 22nd involves a fusion of traits derived from the root number 4. While they share characteristics with those born on the 4th or 13th, their personalities uniquely blend attributes from both number 2 and number 4, with a 50% influence from each.

Number 2 Traits:

- Loving and Supportive: Naturally affectionate, cooperative, and helpful, echoing the qualities of number 2.
- Intuition Power: Gifted with intuition, they navigate situations with foresight.

Challenges from Number 2:

- Emotional and Moody: Despite their harmonious nature, they grapple with emotional sensitivity, mood swings, and insecurity.
- Dependency: They may struggle to make independent decisions, often relying on others emotionally.

Number 4 Traits:

- Hardworking and Disciplined: Possessing qualities from number 4, they are hardworking, disciplined, and focused.
- Leadership Traits: Natural leaders who inspire others with intelligence and perseverance.

Challenges from Number 4:

- Stubborn and Inflexible: Displaying stubbornness, inflexibility, and intolerance, sticking rigidly to plans.
- Resistance to Change: Adapting to new circumstances may be challenging, but they prefer meticulous plans.

In summary, those born on the 22nd present a unique combination of strengths and challenges. Their leadership potential, intelligence, and ability to inspire make them stand out, yet navigating emotional sensitivity and resistance to change requires careful consideration.

A Master Builder in its own right, Master Number 22 is recognized as the creator or constructor. With an innate architectural ability, this number manifests in various life aspects, both personal and professional. Possessing a Midas touch, individuals with this number can turn dreams into beautiful realities. Get to know one of the most industrious numbers among the Master Lot!

The enchanting skill:

This diligent number has a flair for building things from the ground up, often being self-made individuals.

Birth Number 31

Understanding those born on the 31st means recognizing a unique mix of traits shaped by the root number 4. Different from individuals born on the 4th, 13th, and 22nd, their character is a dynamic blend of various numbers.

Trait Breakdown:

- Number 3 (30%): Fun-loving, social, and charismatic traits.
- Number 1 (20%): Pioneering, courageous, determined, and self-motivated attributes.

- Number 4 (50%): Hardworking, disciplined, organized, and focused qualities.

Distinct Features:

- Energetic and Lively: Known for their zest for life, they exude energy and vibrancy.
- Social Connectivity: Natural ability to connect with diverse people, showcasing a friendly demeanor.
- Creative Vision: Innate creativity and imagination, excelling in artistic endeavors, and problem-solving.
- Leadership and Determination: Strong-willed, determined, and exhibiting leadership qualities.
- Intellectual Curiosity: Thirst for knowledge, intellectually curious, always eager to learn.

Relationship Challenges:

- Stubbornness and Inflexibility: Practical and disciplined, but stubbornness may pose challenges.
- Independence: Preferring to live life on their terms, valuing independence.

Conclusion:

People born on the 31st are dynamic and multifaceted. This number combines qualities such as social prowess, creativity, and unwavering determination to create a personality that strives for success and continuous development.

Famous Celebrities with Number 4

- Disha Patani - June 13, 1992
- Anil Ambani - June 4, 1959
- Preity Zinta - January 31, 1975
- Amit Shah - October 22, 1964

- Chetan Bhagat - April 22, 1974
- Isaac Newton - January 4, 1643
- Taylor Swift - December 13, 1989
- Robert Downey Jr. - April 4, 1965
- Rajkummar Rao - August 31, 1984

Good Qualities of Number 4

An individual with the number 4 is influenced by Uranus (Rahu). They possess a strong personality, effective communication skills, and leadership qualities. Number 4 signifies traits such as secrecy, mysticism, a sharp mind, excellent memory, boldness, out-of-the-box thinking, meticulousness, and a critical nature. People with this number often have a rebellious disposition, are oppositional, lack tolerance, and exhibit a rigid attitude. Despite being focused and disciplined, they are also known for their helpful nature and persuasive abilities.

Qualities to improve upon for Number 4

They are very stubborn and inflexible; they don't listen to others, nor do they prefer taking advice from others; they think they know everything and are self-sufficient, it becomes difficult for them to adapt to changes; they sometimes have box thinking and are not open to new ideas and advice; they are intolerant and can become dominating at times; they want things to happen their way and cannot tolerate interference from others; they are very shrewd and can be manipulative sometimes; and they can also lie or trick people to get their work done.

Ruling Planet and Qualities of Ruling Planet for Number 4

Number 4 is linked to Rahu, a powerful planet in the Navagrahas. People born on the 4th, 13th, 22nd, or 31st of any month have Rahu as their ruling planet. Rahu, a shadow planet in Hindu astrology, has a significant impact despite not having a physical form. In Hindu mythology, Rahu is connected to the demon Svarbhanu, and its head became Rahu. Known for creating illusions and desiring material gains, Rahu represents the mind. People influenced by Rahu are knowledgeable, energetic, and confident leaders with sharp memories. However, they may also show rebellious and overconfident traits, leading to negative outcomes.

Rahu is often seen as negative, capable of causing confusion, depression, and emotional imbalance when placed unfavourably in a horoscope. If the number 4 appears three times or more in a person's chart, Rahu's energy might be disturbed, resulting in materialism, manipulation, and deception. A disrupted Rahu can lead to unexplained health issues, mental health challenges, anxiety, or depression. Rahu's influence brings constant ups and downs, sudden wealth, or unexpected problems. Termed a magician, Rahu creates illusions and mysteries, adding to the dynamic nature of those influenced by them.

They prefer control, resist others' opinions, and may face career hurdles. Rahu is a practical and intellectual sign, but its inhabitants can also be obstinate, intolerable, and manipulative. They may encounter obstacles in their careers, dislike change, and prefer to be in charge. Rahu's influence is linked to addictive behaviours like alcoholism or drug addiction. A disturbed Rahu can make individuals aggressive, eccentric, and stubborn, potentially hindering various aspects of their lives. As Rahu is depicted as a head without a body, it remains unsatisfied, always craving more materialistic desires, fame, and success, often characterized by greed and obsessive behaviour.

Weekday ruled by Number 4

Number 4 is guided by Rahu, and although Rahu doesn't have a specific day, Saturday is considered its day. Since numbers 4 and 8 are similar and complementary, Saturday is associated with number 4. Rahu and Shani are somewhat similar in planetary stories. Saturday borns are industrious, self-disciplined, focused, disciplined, pragmatic, and financially astute.

Their innate leadership abilities and insatiable curiosity propel them towards achievement.

Those born on Saturday are known for their high level of discipline and strong work ethic. They are willing to put in extra effort to achieve their goals, showing responsibility and reliability. These individuals earn respect for their diligence and commitment, displaying excellent organizational skills. While confident, intelligent, and knowledgeable, Saturday-born individuals have a practical approach to life, learning from their experiences.

Despite their serious demeanor, Saturday-born people may seem reserved, but those who know them closely find them to be wonderful individuals. They are, however, less comfortable working in groups and may struggle in new environments with unfamiliar people.

Zodiac sign for Number 4

Numerology reveals insights into the unique traits of different zodiac signs, associating each sign with a specific number. For Aquarius, ruled by Rahu, the number 4 aligns with its characteristics.

Aquarians, born between January 21st and February 20th, share traits with those influenced by the number 4: progressive, innovative, and rebellious. Their uniqueness, intellectual curiosity, and self-reliance reflect the qualities of the number 4.

Rahu, governing Aquarius, symbolizes innovation, technology, and sudden events, mirroring Aquarians' distinctive attitude and focused approach. They prioritize making a substantial impact, avoiding superficial gossip, and embracing a life full of opportunities.

Rebels at heart, Aquarians resist authority, akin to the number 4. They can be stubborn and hesitant to seek advice, occasionally facing challenges due to their inflexibility. Respecting their need for freedom is crucial, as it is paramount for Aquarians.

Life Path Number 4

Life Path Number 4 is linked to individuals who are practical, sensible, and rational. They are organized, focused, determined, and never give up on their goals. In essence, they can be described by the 3Ds: determined, disciplined, and driven. These qualities, along with their reliability, faithfulness, and grounded nature, make them respected figures in society.

However, those with Life Path Number 4 may expect high levels of perseverance and discipline from others. Their level-headed and committed approach helps them achieve significant success.

Bill Gates, the renowned business tycoon and founder of Microsoft, is a notable example of Life Path Number 4. Born on October 28, 1955, Gates epitomizes the qualities of this number.

Life Path Number- $2+8+1+0+1+9+5+5= 31= 3+1= 4$

Bill Gates is not only one of the richest individuals globally but also a prominent philanthropist. His relentless work ethic and commitment to constant learning align with the traits of a Life Path 4 person. Gates, known for his analytical mind and ambitious goals, has described himself as incredibly competitive. His dedication to optimization, rather than merely inspiring, reflects his mindset.

Bill Gates' (founder of Microsoft) success aligns with the ideal career path for those with Life Path Number 4, emphasizing the impact of numerology on individual achievements.

Careers for Number 4

Career Alignment with Numerology: Number 4

- A powerful number governed by Rahu, symbolizing sharp-mindedness, intelligence, focus, discipline, organization, and materialism.

Ideal Careers for Number 4 Individuals:

Law and Judiciary:
- Detail-oriented nature suits roles in law, such as those of lawyers, attorneys, and judges.

Finance and Money:
- Strong analytical skills make them apt for finance, trading, banking, and economics.

Politics:
- Sharp intellect and manipulative skills can lead to success in politics.

IT and Technology:
- Success in engineering, manufacturing, and technology is facilitated by technical aptitude

Entrepreneurship:
- Innovative thinking fosters success as entrepreneurs.

Addiction-Related Business:
- Connection to Rahu may lead to success in tobacco or liquor businesses.

Science and Research:
- Intellectual and analytical skills contribute to success in science and research.

Management and Leadership:
- Excellent planning and organizational skills make them successful in managerial roles.

Manual Labor and Craftsmanship:

- Proficiency in hands-on work suits roles like architects, artisans, and carpenters.

Versatility in Jobs and Business:

- Number 4 individuals excel in both jobs and business due to their hard work, intelligence, discipline, determination, and practical approach.

Utilizing Virtues for Success:

- Success for Number 4 individuals lies in directing their skills appropriately, focusing on positive qualities, and strengthening their effects.

People with life path number 4 prefer hard work over shortcuts. A bright future awaits in areas such as banking, management, science, agriculture, and the legal field. Their dedication and productivity make them successful in fruitful and high-yielding endeavours.

Compatibility of Number 4 with other Numbers

Friendly / compatible	Non friendly/ incompatible	Neutral
Friendly numbers are those numbers that will support the energies of number 4 and will enhance its value and make it more positively powerful.	Non-friendly or incompatible numbers conflict with the virtues of number 4, disturb its energies, and bring in struggles in life.	As the name suggests, neutral numbers do not affect the energies of number 4, they neither enhance nor disturb the energies of the number.
4, 5, 6, 7, and 8. (planet wise)	1, 2, 3, and 9. (planet wise)	
1, 4, 6, 7, and 8.	2, 9.	3, 5.

With the help of the above table, we can clearly see the compatibility of number 4 with other numbers and its relationship with them.

Health for Number 4

Understanding Health for Those Born on 4th, 13th, 22nd, and 31st:

1. Rahu's Impact on Health:
   - Governed by Rahu, connected to the mind.
   - Prone to mental health issues like depression, stress, and anxiety.
2. Melancholia and Unexplainable Ailments:
   - Experience melancholia even in joyful moments.
   - Prone to challenging-to-diagnose unexplainable diseases.
3. Insomnia and Active Minds:
   - Active minds may lead to insomnia; their minds seldom rest.
   - Disturbed Rahu energy can cause hormonal imbalances and psychological disorders.
4. Various Infections and Respiratory Issues:
   - Prone to skin, urinary, cough, and cold infections.
   - Respiratory problems, breathlessness, and back pain may also be prevalent.
5. Epidemic Diseases and Healthy Lifestyle:
   - Susceptible to epidemic diseases.
   - Adopting a healthy lifestyle with a diet rich in green vegetables and fresh fruits is crucial.
6. Recommended Dietary Habits:
   - Include carrot, beetroot, and apple juices in their diet.
   - Herbal teas, green leafy vegetables, and sprouts contribute to overall health.
7. Avoiding Anger and Arguments:
   - Steer clear of anger and arguments.
   - A balanced and calm approach is beneficial for their well-being.

In summary, individuals born on the 4th, 13th, 22nd, and 31st can lead a fulfilling and healthier life by maintaining a healthy lifestyle, incorporating specific dietary habits, and managing mental well-being.

Lucky Colours for Number 4

Number 4 is governed by Rahu, and the colors that symbolize Rahu are dark blue and grey, so the lucky colors for number 4 are grey and dark blue. But if number 4 is already repeated thrice or more in a person's chart, then already the energies of the number are disturbed. We should not aggravate it further by wearing the color associated with it. In this case, we should wear other colors that are favourable for number 4, like green and off white.

Lucky Days for Number 4

Number four is governed by Rahu, and it is associated with Saturday, which is a lucky day for number 4 people. Whether they are elemental or planet remedies, all of the remedies for number 4 are completed on Saturdays. For individuals in position four, Wednesdays and Fridays work well as well.

Lucky Years for Number 4

We need to add up all the digits in a year and reduce it or bring it to a single digit. For example, the year 2024 will be calculated as 2+0+2+4 =8, so the year 2024 comes down to number 8. In a similar way, we will calculate the next few years and see which years are lucky for the people in number 4. The years that are compatible with number 4 will be good for them.

2024 - it comes to 8, which is again a compatible number to 4, so this year will also be good for the person. Number 8 is connected to power, and hard work, so it is time to work hard, but the year will also give results of that hardship.

2029- it comes to number 13/4. Since it is a number 4 year, karmic will be good for number 4 people.

2030- It comes to number 5. Since it is a number 5 year, it will be good for number 4 people, as 5 is the most compatible for number 4.

2031, 2032, and 2033 will also be good for number 4.

Lucky Name Number for Number 4

Name number four for personal names is not considered a good number as it makes the person cautious, suspicious, and too stubborn.

Number 4 is also connected to Rahu, which is a malefic planet and can bring unexpected and sudden incidents into your life, so 4 is also a number to be avoided for personal name number.

But in case of business, a company's name can be kept on number four if the company is an IT company or is dealing in any other kind of Technical thing, Name number 4 is also good for companies doing business in liquor or tobacco. Real estate businesses can also keep their company name on number 4. But for an individual's name, one should always avoid number 4.

Other numbers lucky as personal name numbers for number 4 people are 5 and 6.

Remedies for Number 4

There are various types of remedies for increasing the positive impact of number four and decreasing the negative effects of the number. As we all know, number 4 is governed by Planet Rahu, so all the remedies that we take to cure Rahu will also impact the energies of number 4.

Elemental Remedies/Missing Number 4 Remedies

Should an individual's chart lack the number four, incorporating the energies of this sign into their life will require the application of elemental remedies. Since number 4 is related to element wood as per Chinese numerology, the individual needs to bring the energy of wood into his life.

One can wear wooden bracelets, use any wooden pendants, or even use wooden pens to bring the energy of wood into their lives.

Repetitive Number 4 Remedies

If number 4 is repeated more than three times in a person's chart, then definitely the energies of that number and its governing planet are disturbed, so we need to perform following rituals that will reduce the negative effect of the number:

Donate black sesame oil (til ka tel) on Saturdays.

Avoid black, grey, and dark blue clothes.

Planet Remedies for Number 4/ Rahu

The presiding deity for Rahu is Lord Ganesha; whoever's' Rahu is disturbed should worship Ganeshji every day.

They can also feed black dogs to lessen the effect of negative Rahu.

The person can also chant Durga Chalisa on Wednesdays to reduce the malefic effect of Rahu.

Rahu Yantra can also be used to bring prosperity and wealth.

Mantra Remedies

Chant Rahu mantra "Om Rahave Namah" 108 times on Saturdays.

Beej Mantra Remedies

Chant Beej mantra of Rahu, "Om Aing Hring Rahave Namah," 108 times on Saturdays to bring in positive energies of the planet.

Lucky Gemstone

In the case of number 4, which is governed by planet Rahu, the person can wear Hessonite or Gomed. But it is recommended to wear gemstones after consultation with any astrologer.

Bonus Section

Lucky Mobile Number

Number four, as we all know, is governed by Rahu, which is considered a malefic planet, so number four is also treated as a negative number sometimes, so generally it is not suggested to use no. 4 as a mobile number, but some people, like politicians, builders, or people dealing in real estate, can use mobile number 4. On the business front, IT industries or alcohol or tobacco businesses can use mobile number 4 as their official numbers, but in general, number four should be avoided for mobile numbers as it is a number that is associated with struggle, delay, hardship, and sudden incidents.

Lucky mobile numbers for number 4 people are mobile numbers that add up to 5 and 6.

Lucky House Number

Any house number like 58, 31 or A-30 or B-20 all add up to House number 4, which stands for stability, responsibility, and discipline. The energy of house number four is positive, and it encourages the inhabitants to maintain discipline, be organized, grounded, and responsible.

House number four also carries the energies that are required for being rooted and focused; this house number will bring stability and sturdiness to the lives of the people staying in this house. This house number is also a good option for a home office.

However, those who enjoy change and freedom from routine may feel trapped and uninterested in this house number. House number 4 in numerology is an excellent choice if you are driven, ambitious, and in pursuit of your goals, though it might make the residents materialistic.

House number 4 is best suited for politicians, architects, real estate developers, bankers, accountants, engineers, craftsmen and IT professionals.

Lucky Vehicle Number

Vehicle number four promises the person a smooth ride in life devoid of any serious breakdowns on and off the road.

Vehicle number four is not designed for fast driving on roads. Number 4 is also related to wealth and prosperity, so Vehicle number 4 can be lucky for people whose life path number or root number is compatible with number 4, but because number 4 is connected to Rahu, it can cause unexpected issues in the car or delays.

Synopsis

Numerology Number 4: The Foundation of Stability

In the realm of numerology, the number 4 stands as a symbol of stability, practicality, and a strong foundation. Governed by the planet Rahu, individuals born on the 4th, 13th, 22nd, and 31st of any month embody the traits associated with this number.

Grounded and well-mannered, they demonstrate resoluteness and intention in their pursuits, never giving up on obstacles. Rahu's influence bestows intelligence, a keen mind, and a materialistic orientation. These individuals excel in detail-oriented fields like law, finance, and technology, showcasing their analytsical prowess.

However, the shadowy nature of Rahu brings potential challenges, such as mental health issues and a susceptibility to infections. Despite this, by embracing a healthy lifestyle and managing their active minds, those embodying the energy of number 4 can build a resilient and prosperous life.

Co-Authored by - Inndrani Yadav and Vibha Sahu

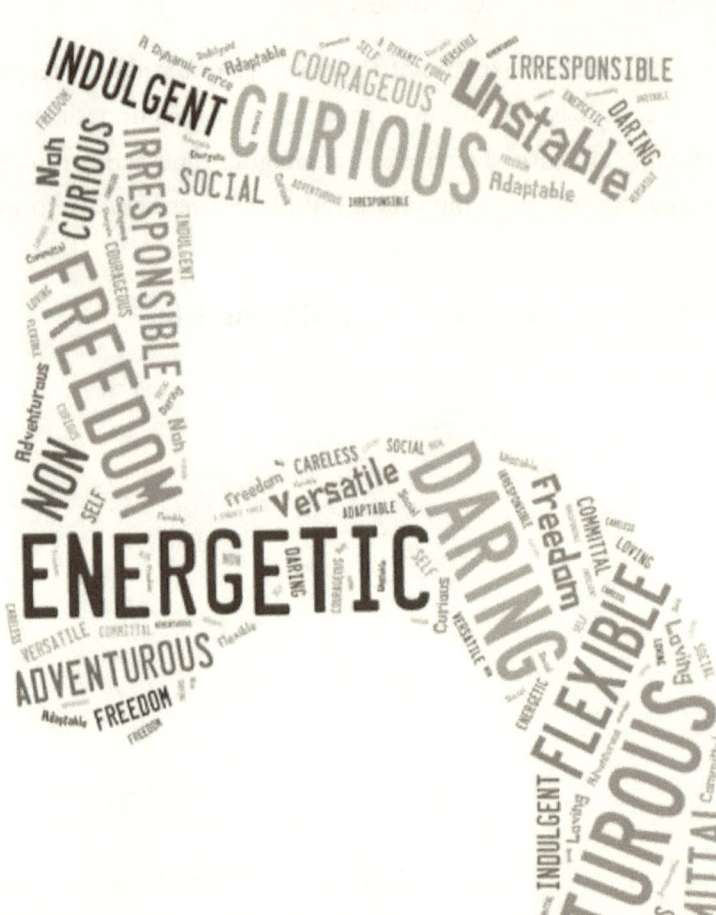

THE NUMBER 5

Root Number 5

According to numerology, those who are born on the 5th, 14th, or 23rd of any month have root number 5. Root is the sum of a person's date of birth, i.e., 5 (5), 14 (1+ 4 = 5), and 23 (2 + 3 = 5). Thus, we see that a person born on the 5th, 14th, or 23rd of any month has a root number 5.

Birth Number 5:

The number 5 is associated with versatility, curiosity, and freedom. People with this root number tend to be adaptable, adventurous, and energetic. They often seek change and variety, and they may have a restless nature that drives them to explore different experiences.

Birth Number 14:

The number 14 1is a combination of the root numbers 1 and 4, and it symbolizes a harmonious blend of leadership and practicality. Individuals with this root number are seen as both ambitious and grounded. They possess leadership qualities and the ability to take initiative, while also being practical and resourceful in their approach to life. This number can indicate success through hard work and determination.

Birth Number 23:

The number 23 is a powerful number associated with creativity, communication, and self-expression. People with this birth number often have a strong sense of individuality and a desire to share their unique ideas and perspectives. They may be naturally creative and have a gift for communication, which could lead to success in artistic or intellectual pursuits.

Famous celebrities

People who are born on 5th, 14th or 23rd of any month constitute the root number 5.

Famous people with root number 5
- Cristiano Ronaldo, February 5, 1985
- Max Gale, April 5, 1943
- Abhishek Bachchan, February 5, 1976
- Dilip Kumar, October 5, 1936.
- Albert Einstein, March 14, 1879
- Aamir Khan, March 14, 1965
- Rohit Shetty, March 14, 1973.
- Kangana Ranaut, March 23, 1987
- Smriti Irani, March 23, 1972
- Gayatri Devi, May 23, 1919.

Good Qualities of Number 5

The Significance of Number 5 in Numerology

The number 5 holds unique qualities that shape the character of those influenced by it:

Adventurous and Dynamic:
- Known for their adventurous spirit and love for excitement.
- Thrive on variety and may feel restless in routine environments.

Freedom-Loving:
- Value freedom and independence.
- Resist being tied down by limitations, preferring personal liberty.

Versatile and Resourceful:
- Naturally versatile and adaptable.
- Possess a range of talents, excel in different areas, and find creative solutions.

Sociable and Charismatic:
- Social butterflies with excellent communication skills.
- Easily connect with people from various backgrounds,

Love for Adventure and Change:
- Inclined towards adventure and change, open to risks and new experiences.
- Thrive in dynamic environments and seek excitement and variety.

Progressive and Forward-Thinking:
- Possess progressive and forward-thinking attitudes.
- Open-minded, receptive to new ideas, and driven by curiosity and a thirst for knowledge.

Qualities to improve upon for Number 5

Restless and Impulsive:
- Prone to restlessness and impulsiveness due to the energy of the number 5.
- May face challenges in focusing and committing to long-term endeavours.

People whose root number is five tend to be multitasking and constantly changing, which limits them. This propensity makes it difficult for them to concentrate on a single task, which causes mood swings and makes finishing tasks challenging. Their scattered thinking involves unravelling multiple thoughts, making them unreliable and prone to unpredictable behaviour.

Their love for freedom can create chaos in both their personal and professional lives. Over-speaking at times may result in people talking senselessly, affecting their interactions with others. Their impatience, overconfidence turning into pride, and excessive ambition can lead to negative consequences, including depression. It is advised that they steer clear of these vices.

Ruling Planet and Qualities of Ruling Planet for Number 5

Root number 5 is associated with the planet Mercury, known for its calm and gentle nature, symbolizing intelligence and cleverness. Mercury, a fast-moving planet, eclipses others and represents balance. Wednesday is the day assigned to Mercury and the number 5. In numerology, 5 is considered the aspiring king, often referred to as the Prince.

Communication: Mercury is frequently linked to wit, intelligence, and communication. Mercury-influenced people typically have sharp minds and excellent communication skills.

Adaptability: Mercury is known for its versatility and adaptability. Individuals with strong Mercury influence are often able to adapt to various situations and thrive in changing environments.

Curiosity: Mercury encourages a curious and inquisitive nature. People with a strong Mercury influence are often interested in learning and exploring new ideas.

Flexibility: Mercury's energy is flexible and dynamic. Those who are receptive to various viewpoints and methods may exhibit these attributes.

Nervous Energy: Mercury's influence can also lead to nervousness and restlessness. People with prominent Mercury traits might find it challenging to relax and might overthink or worry.

Expression: Mercury rules over communication, so those influenced by it might excel in writing, speaking, or other forms of expression.

When combined with the qualities of number 5, which include adaptability, curiosity, and a desire for freedom and exploration, the influence of Mercury further enhances these traits. Mercury is the ruling planet of the number 5, so those who have this sign may be good communicators, love learning, and do well in circumstances requiring quick thinking and flexibility.

Weekday ruled by Number 5

People with the root number 5 find Wednesday to be their special day.

Zodiac sign for Number 5

Number 5 rules over Gemini (born approximately May 21 - June 20) and Virgo (born approximately August 23 - September 22) Zodiac signs. Individuals born under these signs may feel the influence of the number 5 in different facets of their characteristics and life journeys.

Life Path Number 5

Life path number 5 individuals, known as "Fives," embody the spirit of adventure in numerology. They possess inquisitive minds and a deep longing for freedom. Fives resist being confined to a single location, relationship, or concept, recognizing the inevitability of change in life. Despite their captivating and enjoyable nature, their restlessness might lead to unreliability and flakiness. When thriving, Fives showcase qualities of persuasion, outgoingness, and a free-spirited approach. On the flip side, their less favourable traits include a tendency to gossip, a lack of commitment, and inconsistency.

The fortunate number for our country's Prime Minister, Shri Narendra Modi, is 5. His birth date is 17/09/1952, and the total sum of the dates adds up to the number 5. This lucky number, 5, symbolizes a path to success. In his early days, he started a tea stall, later joined RSS, became a member of BJP, entered politics, and actively served, ultimately becoming the Chief Minister of Gujarat and currently holding the position of Prime Minister of India for the second term. His success and unique working style are greatly impacted by the significance of his lucky number, 5.

People with a life path number of five provide insights into the qualities that shape their life's purpose. The individual's life path number, whether constituted from 14 to 5 or 23, has varying effects on their lives and visions of life purposes.

Take Angelina Jolie, born on June 4, 1975, for example. Her life path number is 5, calculated from the number 32 (3 + 2). Angelina is well-known for her appreciation of freedom and for her enjoyment of travel, discovery, and meeting new people. She is driven by her curiosity to explore every new facet of life, and she enjoys working on several projects at once as long as she isn't limited to just one. Angelina easily makes friends, inspiring and attracting people from all walks of life. Gifted with words, she possesses an uncanny ability to inspire others. All these traits collectively highlight her excellence in embodying the qualities associated with the number 5.

Karmic Number

If you're born on the 5th, 14th, or 23rd of any month, your root number is 5. Among these, 14 is considered a karmic number, reflecting bad karma from past lives.

Karmic numbers indicate negative influences from past actions. In the case of Karmic number 14, it suggests that the individual misused freedom in a previous life, was influenced by ego and selfishness, and fell into the trap of addiction. They may have failed because they neglected their obligations to their friends and family, which made it difficult for them to express their emotions and adjust to new situations in their lives.

Karmic numbers, like 14, indicate the repercussions of past life actions in the present. Individuals born on the 14th may face challenges related to discipline, goal-setting, potential addictive behaviours, lack of focus, and poor management skills. They may have a tendency to travel without fruitful outcomes and be adept at many things but master none.

To overcome the adverse effects of the karmic number, individuals are advised to distance themselves from ego and intoxication, maintain discipline, fulfil responsibilities towards family and society, and strive for their happiness.

They need to cultivate discipline, enhance qualities associated with number 4 (such as management), follow a routine, set clear goals, maintain focus, and channel their multitasking abilities in both personal and professional realms. By doing so, they can move towards success in this life.

Careers for Number 5

Individuals with root number 5 have the flexibility to pursue either a job or a business. However, they tend to find more success in business ventures. They have the potential to become successful business owners, leveraging their convincing power and versatile skills.

Number 5 individuals crave stimulation and cannot endure repetitive tasks that lack autonomy, challenge, and change. Due to this, they may opt for self-employment or establish multiple sources of income. Alternatively, they may be drawn to careers that provide adrenaline rushes, such as being a pilot, an ER doctor, or a crisis worker. They might also choose professions that allow them to travel the world.

Number 5 individuals excel in roles related to sales, marketing, and public relations, making these paths highly successful for those with a life path number of five. Career options for individuals with number 5 as their root number include becoming an advocate, writer, travel agent, or entering the marketing field.

They thrive in various fields such as the tourism department, insurance, banking, irrigation, teaching, journalism, astrology, marketing, telecommunications, music, and politics.

For Number 5 individuals searching for their next opportunity, it's advisable to schedule interviews on Wednesday or Friday.

Compatibility of Number 5 with other Numbers

Friend Numbers / Enemy Numbers:
- Friend Numbers (Root 5): 1, 3, 5, 6, 8.
- Enemy Numbers (Root 5): 2, 9.
- Spontaneous Nature: Frolicsome Number 5 is more inclined towards spontaneity than scheduled activities, adventure travel, and excitement over traditional settings.
- Romantic Inclinations: In romantic relationships, a Number 5 is adventurous and seeks intimacy anywhere and everywhere. However, they may exhibit restlessness in committed relationships.
- Loyalty: Despite their restless nature, a Number 5 is known to be a loyal partner once committed. However, prior to reaching that commitment, they might be more unpredictable.

Relationship Compatibility:
- Harmony with 1, 3, and 7: Life path numbers 1, 3, and 7 are seen as compatible with 5.
- With Number 1: Admiration for courage and bravery, but potential clashes due to the desire for control.

- With Number 3: Shared creativity and spontaneity, building a foundation of friendship. However, there might be challenges with focus and reliability.
- Adaptability and Compatibility with 4 (Rahu): Number 5's adaptability makes it best friends with number 4, associated with Rahu. Rahu is a planet, symbolizing unpredictability and change. The adaptable nature of 5 allows it to resonate well with the energies of Rahu, leading to a harmonious relationship. This adaptability helps 5 navigate the unpredictable and sometimes chaotic influence of Rahu.
- Synergy with 6: Number 6 is considered a great companion for 5. The nurturing and stable qualities of 6 balance the adventurous and spontaneous nature of 5. Together, they create a dynamic partnership where the caring nature of 6 complements the free-spirited energy of 5.
- With Number 7: Balance of intimacy and independence, understanding each other's need for alone time, and complementing strengths and weaknesses.
- Strong Bonds with 8: Number 8 is another favourable companion for 5. The desire for accomplishment and success is shared by both numbers. The bold and aspirational characteristics of 8 complement the spirit of adventure of 5. Their combined energies can lead to productive collaborations and shared goals.

Understanding these deeper dynamics with numbers enhances insights into the social and relational aspects of individuals with a life path number 5. It highlights the intricate interplay of energies and characteristics that contribute to the overall compatibility and dynamics of their relationships.

In contrast, Number 5 might not find as much compatibility with 2 and 9. Understanding these dynamics can help individuals with life path number 5 navigate their relationships more effectively.

Health for Number 5

People with the root number 5 may face health issues primarily connected to the stomach. Disturbed energy or imbalance in the number 5 could lead to problems such as

Injuries and Accidents: Due to their adventurous spirit, number 5 individuals might engage in riskier activities. Being cautious and safety-conscious can help prevent accidents and injuries.

Overindulgence: Number 5 individuals are known for enjoying the pleasures of life, which might lead to overindulgence in food, drink, or other substances. Moderation and a balanced lifestyle are important.

Digestive Issues: The 5's love for variety might lead to inconsistent eating habits. This can result in digestive problems. Maintaining a balanced diet and eating at regular intervals can help.

Nervous System Concerns: The highly active mind of a number 5 person might lead to nervousness and anxiety. Engaging in calming activities like yoga and meditation can help balance their nervous system.

Respiratory Issues: Number 5 individuals might be prone to respiratory issues due to their active lifestyle. Avoiding exposure to pollutants and maintaining respiratory health are important.

Attention Span: With a tendency to seek new experiences, number 5 individuals might struggle with maintaining focus for extended periods. Developing mindfulness practices can aid concentration.

Sleep Patterns: Restlessness can affect sleep patterns. Establishing a consistent sleep routine and creating a relaxing bedtime environment can improve sleep quality.

Lucky Colours for Number 5

People with the root number 5 are recommended to embrace certain colours for good luck. To attract positive energy, individuals with the root number 5 are advised to incorporate shades of Green and khaki, milky white, orange, yellow, and light blue into their clothing, as well as items like pillows, cushion covers, curtains, tablecloths, bed sheets, and more.

Lucky Numbers for Number 5

The friendly and compatible numbers for Number 5 are 1, 3, 4, 5, 6, 7, 8. Number 2 and Number 9 are the only numbers that have an unfriendly relationship with Number 5.

Lucky Days for Number 5

For those with the root number 5, specific days are seen as extra lucky, aligning well with the lively energy of the number 5. Wednesdays, influenced by Mercury, the ruling planet, are especially auspicious, enhancing qualities like adaptability and communication. Fridays, associated with Venus, also bring favourable vibes, promoting social interactions and creativity.

Lucky Years for Number 5

The most favourable years in the lives of individuals with root number 5 are the 5th, 14th, 23rd, 32nd, 41st, 50th, 59th, 68th, 77th, and 86th. These are the years when they may experience unexpected financial growth, career advancements, marriage, the joy of children, or other favourable events.

Your personal year number for your which aligns with the energy of the number 5, can also be favourable.

To calculate the Personal Year Number, add the digits of your Birth date and Birth Month to the current year.

For example, if you were born onJanuary 1 and the current year is 2024, the calculation would be: 1+ 1 + 2 + 0 + 2 + 4 = 10/1. So, for 2024, your personal year number would be 1.

Years when the Universal Year Number aligns with the energy of the number 5 can also be favourable. Additionally, any year that adds up to the numbers 1, 5, or 6 is particularly auspicious, signalling favourable circumstances and opportunities.

To calculate the Universal Year Number, add the digits of the current year. For example, if the year is 2024, the calculation would be:

2 + 0 + 2 + 4 = 8. So, 2024 would be a Universal year 8.

So next 5 lucky years for number 5 Individuals are:

2024= 2+0+2+4 = 8

2026=2 + 0 + 2 + 6 = 10 = 1 + 0 = 1.

2028=2 + 0 + 2 + 8 = 12 = 1 + 2 = 3.

2030=2 + 0 + 3 + 0 = 5.

2031=2 + 0 + 3 + 1 = 6.

Lucky Name Number for Number 5

Individuals with a name number of five are recognized for their exceptional talent and versatility. This name number endows them with the diverse qualities associated with the number 5, propelling them to great heights.

For those with root number 5, the most fortunate name numbers are those whose total sum is 1, 5, or 6. It is essential to ensure that both the first name and full name align with these auspicious numbers for maximum positive impact.

However, it is to be ensured that the total of the first name number or total name number is not a karmic number i.e. 14.

Remedies for Number 5

Elemental Remedies

To address the absence or deficiency of the number 5 in one's numerology chart, individuals can consider a remedy by wearing anything connected to the element earth as per feng-shui like crystal necklace or bracelet. It is thought that the stone contains particular vibrations or energies that coincide with the qualities connected to the number 5.

The goal of this remedy is to introduce and strengthen the attributes associated with the number 5, which include flexibility, adaptability, and a love of independence. Wearing the crystal serves as a symbolic and energetic way to invite the influence of the missing number into one's life, promoting balance and completeness in their personal energies.

Planet Remedies

Remedies associated with the planet for individuals with numerology number 5 include:

1. Green Colour Usage:
   - Individuals with the number 5 are advised to incorporate the colour green into their surroundings as much as possible.
   - Wearing green clothing, using green accessories, or decorating living spaces with green elements are considered beneficial.
   - Additionally, feeding green fodder to a cow on Wednesdays is recommended.
2. Worship of Lord Vishnu:
   - Worshiping Lord Vishnu is suggested as a remedy for those influenced by the energy of number 5.

Mantra Remedies

The mantra associated with the number 5 and the planet Mercury (Budh) is "Om Budhaye Namah." Chanting this mantra is believed to align an individual with the energy of Mercury and bring positive influences associated with the number 5 in numerology.

Beej Mantra Remedies

The Beej Mantra associated with the number 5 and the planet Mercury (Budh) is "Om Braam Breem Braum Sah Budhaya Namah."

Chanting the "Om Braam Breem Braum Sah Budhaya Namah" Beej Mantra with sincerity and focus is believed to bring about the positive influences associated with Mercury, promoting intellectual clarity, effective communication, and overall well-being.

Similar to other Beej Mantras, it is recommended to chant this mantra 108 times.

Lucky Gemstone

Significance of Green Emerald:

- Gem for Mercury (Budh): Green Emerald is associated with the planet Mercury (Budh) in Vedic astrology.
- Symbolizes Communication: Mercury signifies communication, intelligence, and analytical abilities.
- Color Energies: The green colour of Emerald represents freshness, growth, and balance.
- Personalized Advice: Seeking advice from a qualified astrologer ensures that the gem aligns with the individual's astrological profile.

Bonus Section

a) Lucky Mobile Number

If the sum of the digits in the mobile number of someone with root number 5 adds up to 1, 5, or 6, then that mobile number is considered auspicious. It's important to avoid excessive repetition of any digit in the number.

However, make sure that it's not a karmic number, doesn't have any number repeating more than twice, and does not end in zero.

Avoid using a total of 5 for personal use; it's very good for business purposes. To bring harmony and peace to life, use a number totaling 6.

b) Lucky House Number

People residing in a house with the number 5 are likely to experience a lively and fun atmosphere, with good opportunities for those working from home, especially in sales. However, the constant change may bring unexpected results. It could be difficult to find calm in such a home because everyone is constantly thinking and doing different things. If the total sum of the house numbers for someone with root number 5 adds up to 1, 5, or 6, then that house number is considered auspicious.

c) Lucky Vehicle Number

If the sum of the last four digits of a person's vehicle number with root number 5 adds up to 1, 5, or 6, then that vehicle number is considered auspicious. It's important that the vehicle number doesn't have repeated zero digits and is in ascending order. Additionally, the vehicle number should match the name number of the vehicle owner. Having such an auspicious vehicle number is favourable for successful professional trips and overall travel experiences.

Synopsis

People with root number 5 can be considered fortunate, possessing qualities like balance, tact, attractiveness, and cheerfulness. They showcase capabilities in various tasks and, when patient and in good company, are unstoppable on their path to success. To sum up, people with the root number five are vivacious, enthusiastic, and eager to learn about many aspects of the world, people, and society. Those who identify with root number 5 are vibrant, passionate, and eager to learn about many aspects of the world, people, and society. Their versatility, multi-talents, and communication skills make them adaptable in various situations, portraying them as good friends with a humorous and adventurous nature. Their influential presence often marks them as public figures, emphasizing their motto of leading a free life.

Co- Authored By - Rohini Kumar Mahto, Mokshaa Rampal Singh and Vaibbhav Joshi

THE NUMBER 6

THE NUMBER 6

Root Number

The root number is the sum of the digits of the birth date People with root number 6 are born on the 6th, 15th, or 24th of any month.

There are pure numbers and combinations of numbers.

Number 6 is pure if the birth date is 6th, and a combination of other numbers if the birth date is 15th or 24th.

The personality of a person with root number 6 depends on the pure number or combination of numbers they have.

For example, a person born on 6th will have different traits compared to people born on the 15th and 24th.

People born on the 15th have some traits of number 1 and number 5, but mostly of number 6.

Similarly, a person born on the 24th has some traits of number 2 and number 4, but mostly of number 6.

Famous celebrities

Indian Personalities:

A R Rahman—January 6, 1966.

Kapil Dev—January 6, 1959.

Bai Chung Bhutia—December 15, 1976.

APJ Abdul Kalam—February 15, 1931.

Azim Premji—July 24, 1945.

Atal Bihari Vajpayee—December 24, 1924.

International Celebrities:

George w Bush—July 6, 1946

Xi Jinping—June 15, 1953

Steve Jobs—February 24, 1955

Lionel Messi—June 24, 1987.

Good Qualities of Number 6

The efficient Yin energy affects those with root number 6 who were born on the 6th, 15th, or 24th day of any given month. This number is often linked with feminine attributes like compassion, love, and caring.

Characteristics:

1. Family-Centric: Root 6 individuals have a strong sense of family and community and are always ready to help and protect their loved ones.
2. Knowledgeable Advisors: They are knowledgeable and good advisors, offering wise and practical solutions to problems.
3. Love for Learning: They have a keen interest in learning, often leading to opportunities for travel or settling abroad.
4. Realistic and Artistic: Root 6 individuals appreciate beauty, comfort, and luxury in life. They are both realistic and artistic.
5. Cheerful Generosity: Known for their cheerful and generous nature, they carry a positive demeanour and value success and wealth.

Birth Number 15:

1. Balanced Energies: Those born on the 15th have both Yang and Yin energies, exhibiting a positive attitude towards life.
2. Innovative and Creative: They are innovative, creative, and possess leadership qualities with a flair for entrepreneurship.
3. Determined Communicators: Determined and self-motivated, they are good communicators, expressing ideas convincingly.
4. Courageous Multi-Talents: These individuals are courageous, multi-talented, responsible, and capable of handling various situations.

Birth Number 24

1. Sensitivity and Emotion: Individuals born on the 24th have more Yin energy, making them sensitive and emotional.
2. Cooperative and Responsible: They are cooperative, organized, and responsible team players with a strong sense of duty.
3. Motherly Nature: With a motherly nature, their nurturing instincts are even more pronounced than those of pure number 6 individuals.
4. Diplomatic and Tactful: Diplomatic and tactful, they handle conflicts and disagreements with grace and harmony.

Qualities to improve upon for Number 6

Areas for Improvement:

1. Balancing Protection: Root 6 individuals may become excessively protective, neglecting their own needs. Balancing self-care is crucial.
2. Avoiding Self-Centeredness: They should avoid being too self-centred and considerate of others' feelings and opinions.
3. Addressing Negative Traits: Tendencies such as argumentativeness, materialism, selfishness, impatience, and short temper should be acknowledged and addressed.

4. Respecting Boundaries: Root 6 individuals are supposed to be considerate of others' opinions and know the line of boundaries. They should also learn to say no when required.
5. Emotional Control: Controlling emotional impulses and utilizing logic and intuition for better judgement are essential.

Ruling Planet and Qualities of Ruling Planet for Number 6

Venus, the Planet of Love and Beauty

Venus, the planet associated with love in various forms, symbolizes romance, intimacy, luxury, and abundance. Let's explore the characteristics and influences of Venus on individuals.

Characteristics:

1. Aesthetic Sense: People influenced by Venus possess a strong aesthetic sense, appreciating beauty in various forms.
2. Creative Flair: They often have a creative flair. Their creativity flows like a running tap, which allows them to reflect their inner creativity in every facet of life.
3. Fashionable Appearance: Venus-influenced individuals tend to dress well, attracting others with their stylish and appealing attire.
4. Attraction and Charm: It is their innate nature to pull people's attention toward them, like a magnet does with their charm, and they attain happiness in others' company.
5. Love for Beautiful Things: These individuals have a genuine love for beautiful things, seeking pleasure in aesthetics.
6. Fame-Loving and Prosperous: Venus influences a love for recognition and prosperity, contributing to a desire for fame and success.

Relationship Values:

1. Loyalty and Dedication: Individuals influenced by Venus highly value loyalty and dedication in their relationships.

2. **Seeking Peace and Harmony:** Harmony and peace are essential for them, and they actively pursue environments that provide such qualities.
3. **Intolerance for Clumsiness:** They do not tolerate clumsiness, preferring order and grace in their surroundings.
4. **Cleanliness Matters:** Venus-influenced individuals have a low tolerance for filthiness, appreciating cleanliness.

Venus moulds those who actively seek out beauty in all facets of their existence, in addition to simply appreciating it. Venus's influence brings a touch of elegance and aesthetic appreciation to their path, influencing everything from relationships and personal style to success-driven endeavors.

Weekday ruled by number 6

Friday, ruled by Venus and named after Guru Shukracharya, holds a special place in astrology. The qualities associated with Venus, the planet of love and beauty, influence individuals born on this day, even if they do not have the number 6 in their numerology.

Friday's Venusian Qualities:

1. **Grace and Charm:** Individuals born on Friday often exude grace and charm, reflecting Venus's influence. This grace extends to their mannerisms and interactions with others.
2. **Love for Aesthetics:** Venus is closely related to aesthetics, therefore people under the influence of Friday might be more aware of beauty in all its manifestations. This could manifest in an attraction to art, fashion, or a general love for visually pleasing surroundings.
3. **Harmony in Relationships:** Venus is associated with harmony, and people born on Friday may value harmonious relationships. In their relationships with other people, they probably look for harmony and balance.

4. Artistic Inclinations: Friday-born individuals might possess artistic inclinations, expressing creativity in different aspects of their lives. This could manifest in artistic hobbies, a love for creative projects, or an appreciation for artistic endeavours.
5. Sociable Nature: Venus is linked to social connections, and those born on Friday may be naturally sociable. They are the most content when they spend quality time with their acquaintances, and their interactions are likely to be characterized by warmth and friendliness.

In summary, Friday's connection to Venus brings forth qualities of grace, charm, and a love for aesthetics. These individuals, whether consciously or unconsciously, embody the positive attributes associated with Venus, creating a harmonious and creatively enriched life.

Zodiac signs for Number 6

Venus, the planet of love and beauty, holds sway over two zodiac signs: Taurus and Libra. Individuals born under these signs may display certain Venusian qualities, irrespective of their specific birth date.

For those born from April 21 to May 20 (Taurus) and September 21 to October 20 (Libra), certain venusian traits become a part of their character.

In essence, Venus's influence on Taurus and Libra brings forth qualities of beauty appreciation, a desire for harmony, and a natural charm that enhances their interactions and relationships.

Life Path Number 6

The Caring Guardian

If you've ever been seen as the nurturing figure in your group, chances are you resonate with life path number 6. Often considered the "parent" of numerology, sixes embody compassion, nurturing qualities, and a protective instinct for their loved ones' well-being, even if it means taking on a slightly stern demeanor.

The number 6 holds the title of the most harmonios single-digit number in numerology. Its core essence revolves around being the caretaker, embodying love, sacrifice, protection, and a commitment to teaching and healing others. Often referred to as the "motherhood/fatherhood number," the 6 is the adhesive that binds families and communities together.

Creating an environment characterized by peace and harmony is the primary focus of number 6. Its influence is vital for the functioning of families and communities, as it brings people together, fostering a sense of unity and care.

In essence, life path number 6 individuals are the caring guardians who, at their best, provide unwavering support and love, contributing to a harmonious and nurturing environment.

1. At Their Best: Sixes shine when they display reliability, provide unwavering support, and express genuine love. Their nurturing nature creates a harmonious environment for those around them.
2. At Their Worst: In challenging moments, sixes may become self-righteous, overly involved in others' affairs, and occasionally adopt a martyr-like attitude. These traits can lead to conflicts in their relationships.

For example, Virat Kohli, who was born on November 5, 1988, has a life path number of 6. This is because $5 + 1 + 1 + 1 + 9 + 8 + 8 = 33$, which is 6.

It is said that after the age of 35, people are more influenced by their life path number than by their root number.

Virat Kohli shows these traits in his personality, as he is devoted to his family and his team.

As a result of his skill and dedication, he also benefits from wealth and recognition.

However, he may also have some of the challenges of number 6, such as being too selfless or emotional.

He might occasionally put others' wants and feelings ahead of his own desires.

Master Number

Master Number 33 - The Powerful Teacher:

Master numbers are special numbers with higher energy and greater potential compared to regular numbers. One such rare and potent master number is 33.

Master Number 33 - The Exceptional Blend:

Master number 33 is a unique combination of two 3s (linked to Jupiter, the guru of the gods) and 6 (associated with Venus, the guru of the demons). This powerful combination makes 33 one of the most exceptional master numbers.

Qualities of Individuals with Master Number 33:

1. Expressive and Knowledgeable: Those with master number 33 possess the expressive and knowledgeable qualities associated with number 3.
2. Abundant and Compassionate: Infused with the attributes of 6, they embody abundance, luxury, and a compassionate nature.
3. Charismatic and Loving: Key characteristics that make them innately endearing to others are charm and love.
4. Service-Oriented and Spiritually Aware: There's a strong sense of service and a high level of spiritual awareness within individuals with master number 33.

Life Path and Name Number Significance:

Those with the master number 33 as their life path or name number showcase a unique blend of qualities from both 3 and 6. They are not only expressive, creative, and knowledgeable but also abundant, luxurious, and loving.

Life Purpose and Abilities:

1. Born Teachers and Preachers: Individuals with master number 33 are destined to be teachers and preachers, using their wisdom and power to inspire and guide others.
2. Creators of Wonders: With their exceptional talents and abilities, they have the potential to create wonders and exceptions in various aspects of life.

In essence, Master Number 33 individuals are powerful and exceptional beings, possessing qualities that make them both influential leaders and compassionate guides.

Careers for Number 6

Number 6 in Careers: Embracing Love and Beauty

If you have the number 6 in your chart, you're naturally inclined towards careers filled with love, service, harmony, and beauty. If these traits fit your career path, you're headed in the correct direction, regardless of whether you decide to work for yourself or launch your own business.

The number 6 is linked to Venus, the planet of luxury, romance, knowledge, family, and relationships. Individuals with this number tend to be caring, loyal, artistic, and prosperous.

Consider careers in teaching, health services, counselling, local politics, farming, or working with livestock. These professions allow you to share knowledge, assist others, foster harmony, and connect with nature.

If business is your calling, think about ventures related to fashion, luxury, and beauty. These industries resonate with your aesthetic sense, creativity, and prosperity. You can create products or services that bring more beauty, comfort, and joy into people's lives.

Compatibility of Number 6 with other Numbers

Compatibility of numbers is a way to understand how well people with different numbers get along. Number compatibility is based on the qualities and vibrations of each number. Here's a quick look at how Number 6 interacts with others:

1. Numbers 6 and 1:
   - Challenges: Differences in leadership and cooperation.
   - Advice: Understand each other's needs and respect differences.
2. Numbers 6 and 2:
   - Compatibility: Moderately compatible.
   - Balance: Number 2's sensitivity complements Number 6's caring nature.
   - Communication: Clear expression of feelings is key.
3. Numbers 6 and 3:
   - Compatibility: Good match.
   - Shared Interests: Creativity, Joy, and Adventure.
   - Caution: Varied approaches to spontaneity and stability.
4. Numbers 6 and 4:
   - Compatibility: Low.
   - Challenges: Clash in flexibility, organization, and priorities.
   - Solution: Compromise, appreciate strengths and weaknesses.
5. Numbers 6 and 5:
   - Compatibility: Poor.
   - Differences: Stability-seeking vs. adventurous nature.
   - Effort Needed: Flexibility, understanding, and support.
6. Numbers 6 and 6:

- Compatibility: High.
- Similarities: Shared values, family focus.
- Watch Out: Potential for dominance and stubbornness.
7. Numbers 6 and 7:
   - Compatibility: Low.
   - Divergence: Social vs. introspective nature.
   - Action Needed: Nurture with openness and respect.
8. Numbers 6 and 8:
   - Compatibility: Good.
   - Balance: Emotional security meets material security.
   - Challenge: Managing dominance and control.
9. Numbers 6 and 9:
   - Compatibility: Moderate.
   - Altruism Clash: Over-giving tendencies may need balance.
   - Consideration: Different financial views may arise.

Conclusion:

Understanding these dynamics helps foster stronger relationships. Embrace compromises, respect differences, and appreciate each other's strengths and weaknesses.

Health for Number 6

Every number has a corresponding physical system or portion, according to numerology. In this chart, a number can stand for a possible health issue or a strength associated with a specific body part or system; it can also be absent or recurrent. In case of number 6, which represents the reproductive and sexual organs, people who have this number as their root number, life path number, or repeated more than once in their grid may have health issues related to these organs.

They may suffer from PCOD (polycystic ovarian disease), PCOS (polycystic ovary syndrome), gynaecological problems in women, or genital problems in men.

These issues may affect their fertility, sexuality, hormones, mood, and self-esteem.

They may also have health issues related to their nose, throat, and chest, such as allergies, sinusitis, sore throat, cough, cold, bronchitis, or asthma.

These issues may affect their breathing, immunity, communication, and expression.

People should do pranayama and breathing exercises regularly to strengthen their lungs and respiratory system.

They should also include nuts, especially almonds, and beans in their diet to nourish their reproductive and sexual organs.

In order to prevent aggravating their health problems, individuals should also abstain from smoking, drinking, eating spicy food, and stress.

Lucky Colours for Number 6

In numerology, each number has a corresponding colour that resonates with its vibration and meaning.

In case of number 6, the colour represented by Venus, the planet of love, beauty and harmony, is off-white.

Off-white is a soft and soothing colour that symbolizes purity, elegance, peace and balance.

When attending a wedding, job interview, business meeting, or presentation or any other significant event where we must make critical decisions we should wear our lucky hue.

It will make us feel calm, graceful, harmonios, and diplomatic. It will also attract positive people and opportunities toward us.

Lucky Numbers for Number 6

Lucky numbers for 6 are 1, 2, 4, 5, and 6.

Lucky Days for Number 6

Number 6 is governed by the planet Venus. Friday is considered an auspicious day for those under the influence of Venus. This day is associated with love, romance, and aesthetic pleasures. People born under the influence of number 6 may find Fridays particularly favourable for activities related to relationships, creativity, and enjoyment. Wednesdays and Saturdays are also good for number 6.

Lucky Years for Number 6

Lucky years are those years that are calculated based on the Universal year and the personal year.

Lucky years for 6 are:

Year 2024=2+0+2+4=8.

Year 2027=2+0+2+7=11=2.

Year 2029=2+0+2+9=13=4.

Year 2030=2+0+3+0=5.

Year 2031=2+0+3+1=6.

Lucky Name Number for Number 6

When the total of our name digits comes to 6, the person may possess the qualities of number 6, even though they may not be present directly in their chart.

Number 6 represents abundance, knowledge, family, romance, love relations, and harmony.

It is a powerful Yin number, which means it is feminine, passive, receptive, and nurturing.

The energy of 6 is bestowed upon the individual, enabling them to be kind, devoted, creative, prosperous, steady, peaceful, and diplomatic.

We can change the name number to a number compatible with their core numbers.

This can be done by changing or adding some letters to the name to increase its vibration to 6.

When we bring the name number to 6, the person gains the qualities of 6 and attracts more abundance, knowledge, and luxury into their life.

Remedies for Number 6

a) Elemental Remedies

These remedies are taken when a number that denotes one of the elements of the universe is missing in our chart.

The elements are water, earth, wood, metal, and fire.

They represent different aspects of our lives, such as emotions, stability, growth, creativity, and passion.

Missing number 6:

Number 6 is connected to the metal element. Metal represents creativity, intelligence, communication, and prosperity.

If the number 6 is missing in our chart, the elemental remedy is to wear a gold colour metal strap watch.

Repetition of Number 6:

If number 6 is repeated twice, then it makes the person more creative in nature.

If it is repeated more than twice, remedies need to be taken.

In such cases, one should

- Donate sugar, silver, rice, milk, white cloth, ghee, white flowers, incense, perfume, white sandalwood, etc.
- These represent luxury and abundance, and due to repetition, they are creating a negative impact on the person.
- Remedies should be done on Fridays.
- Avoid wearing white and off-white clothes.

b) Planet Remedies

Colour remedies:

To bring in the energies of missing numbers, one can use colour remedies as well. It means either you can wear the colour of the missing number or carry accessories that represent that number and planet.

In case of Number 6, one can wear off-white clothes, especially on Fridays, to bring in the energies and vibrations of number 6.

Yantras:

Number 6 is connected to the planet Venus, which represents love, romance, family, travel, and abundance.

Venus Yantra can be used to enhance our love life, family relations, travel opportunities, and abundance.

c) Mantra Remedies

- Number 6 is connected to the planet Venus, which represents love, romance, family, travel, and abundance.
- The mantra for Venus is Om Shukraya Namah (ॐ शुाय नमः).
- This mantra can be used to please Venus and attract its positive qualities into our lives.

d) Beej Mantra Remedies

For the planet Venus, the Beej mantra is Aum Dram Drim Draum Sah Shukraya Namah.

This mantra should be recited 16000 times over a period of 40 days.

This mantra can be used to reduce the negative effects of Venus in our chart and increase its positive effects.

e) Lucky Gemstone

The diamond is a gemstone that represents the planet Venus. The diamond is a precious stone that symbolizes purity, beauty, elegance, and wealth. It can enhance our love lives, family relations, travel opportunities, and abundance.

The alternative semi-precious gems for Venus are white sapphire and white zircon. They have similar properties as diamonds but are less expensive and more easily available.

The metals related to Venus are silver, white gold, and platinum. They are shiny, smooth, and attractive metals that are capable of enhancing our creativity, intelligence, communication, and prosperity.

Caution: These gemstones should be worn only after consulting a good astrologer.

Bonus Section

a) Lucky Mobile Number

Due to the nature of number 6, which represents abundance, romance, family, and knowledge, it is considered lucky when the total of all the digits summed up comes to number 6 and 5.

b) Lucky House Number

House Number 6 is considered to be fortunate as it represents family, love, romance, and prosperity.

c) Lucky Vehicle Number

A vehicle number that comes to 6 when the total of all the digits is calculated is considered to be good when it is compatible with the person for whose name it is registered.

Synopsis

Number 6 is a powerful and positive number in numerology that represents abundance, knowledge, family, romance, and harmony.

People with number 6 in their chart are usually generous, loyal, loving, creative, and intelligent.

They have a strong sense of responsibility and duty towards their family and society.

They value beauty, art, culture, and harmony. They are often successful in fields that require creativity, communication, diplomacy, and service.

Co- Authored By Vishalli Sreeppada

THE NUMBER 7

THE NUMBER 7

Root Number

Numbers That Come Under The Category Of Root Number

People born on 7th, 16th, and 25th of any month are governed by the number 7, and the number is connected to planet Ketu in numerology.

Famous celebrities

Indian Celebrities

Rabindra Nath Tagore – May 7, 1861.

Mahendra Singh Dhoni – July 7, 1981.

Katrina Kaif – July 16, 1983.

Karan Johar – May 25, 1972.

International Celebrities

Queen Elizabeth – September 7, 1533.

Charlie Chaplin – April 16, 1889.

Nick Jonas – September 16, 1992.

Sir Isaac Newton – December 25, 1642.

Good Qualities of Number 7

Individuals characterized by root number 7 exhibit a multifaceted nature, combining intellectual acumen with a penchant for investigation. Their intuitive faculties are finely tuned, allowing them to approach challenges with a sense of calm and a methodical, analytical mindset. Moreover, their affinity for technical pursuits adds an extra layer of depth to their unique qualities.

Qualities to improve upon for Number 7

While individuals with root number 7 in numerology are associated with many positive qualities, there are always areas for personal growth and improvement.

For individuals with root number 7, it's beneficial to work on cultivating qualities such as open-mindedness, transparency, optimism, trust, and empathy. Extending these qualities can result in greater communication, stronger bonds with others, and a more optimistic view of life. People can establish a more harmonious and meaningful life, both personally and collectively, by letting go of intolerance, secrecy, cynicism, pessimism, and distrust.

Ruling Planet and Qualities of Ruling Planet for Number 7

In numerology, the ruling planet of the number 7 is Ketu. Ketu is the headless body of the asura, Svarbhanu, and it represents the southern lunar node. Ketu is responsible for the eclipse of the moon, where the deity is said to completely swallow the lunar celestial body. The Navagraha is depicted without a head, with four arms and a serpent's tail instead of legs, mounted on his vahana, a vulture.

Individuals with this ruling planet possess a unique blend of spiritual depth, imaginative creativity, psychic sensitivity, and a quest for higher knowledge. They are intuitive seekers who often excel in creative and intellectual pursuits while also harbouring a profound connection to the mystical and unseen aspects of existence. Balancing their dreamy idealism with practicality is key to fully realizing their potential.

Weekday ruled by Number 7

Rahu and Ketu, being shadow planets, don't have a dedicated day assigned to them. However, in astrology, Rahu is linked to Saturn, and Ketu to Mars. Because of these resemblances, Tuesday, which is ruled by Mars, is also seen as a noteworthy day for Ketu, in line with the impact of the number 7.

Zodiac sign for Number 7

Ketu, one of the lunar nodes in Vedic astrology, governs the zodiac sign Scorpio in conjunction with Mars (Mangala) as it is exactly like Mars. According to this astrological association, people who were born under the sign of Scorpio might be influenced by Ketu, which would add special traits and energy to their astrological nature. The alignment of Ketu and Mars in Scorpio can influence various aspects of a person's personality, behaviours, and life events, as interpreted within the framework of Vedic astrology. So indirectly, number 7 rules over Zodiac Scorpio with Mars.

Life Path Number 7: Unravelling the Mystery

Life Path Number 7 individuals possess an intriguing air of mystery. They often seem like keepers of secret knowledge, whether acquired through extensive research or their heightened intuition. Preferring the company of books over people, these individuals are natural scholars, driven by a desire to comprehend the depths of everything around them. When stress arises, finding solace in nature becomes crucial for sevens.

At their best:

Analytical, spiritual, and wise, sevens shine when immersed in deep thought and exploration.

At their worst:

They may exhibit traits of secrecy, aloofness, and pessimism during challenging times.

The Philosopher's Path:

The essence of number 7 lies in seeking, thinking, and searching for truth. As philosophers in numerology, Sevens don't accept things at face value. They constantly strive to unveil hidden truths, recognizing that reality often lurks behind illusions.

The 7 is special because their mind is both their best tool and their biggest limitation. They are logical, flexible, and always eager to learn, taking their thoughts to places others rarely do. With a vast and powerful imagination, they explore spiritual realms others may never discover. While the 7 delves deep, they stay intellectual and rational.

Their joy in mental exploration lets them appreciate long hours alone. However, they rely heavily on the power of the mind, limiting their ability to truly experience life, which comes from living, not just thinking or speaking.

Let's understand this with an example of a celebrity with a life path number 7.

Madhuri Dixit, a renowned Indian actress, has a life path number of 7. Her birth date is May 15, 1967.

Calculation: $1 + 5 + 5 + 1 + 9 + 6 + 7 = 34$.

Life Path Number: $3 + 4 = 7$.

Madhuri Dixit, with a Life Path Number 7, embodies a blend of intellect, spirituality, creativity, and intuition. Her journey as an actress and public figure may be marked by a constant quest for knowledge, a deep appreciation for introspection, and a unique ability to infuse her performances with a distinct combination of intellectual depth and artistic flair. Her hunger for learning new things and extra attentiveness could act as the concrete base for her immense success and versatility in the entertainment industry, while her inner world of introspection and spirituality could serve as a source of inspiration and resilience throughout her career and life journey.

Karmic Number 16/7

Karmic debt number 16 (1 + 6 = 7): The number 16 relates to past life wrongdoing when it comes to love. This could manifest as repeated cycles of having your heart broken or breaking others' hearts. It's important to address toxic relationship patterns and commit to honesty and loyalty.

The 16 karmic debt means destruction of the old and birth of the new. It is about the fall of the ego and all it has built for itself.

The Abuse of Love: The karmic debt of the 16/7 arises from past involvement in illicit love affairs that caused suffering to others: In some manner, love was abused. Quite simply, the 16/7 indicates a failure in the past to act responsibly in matters of love.'

Number 16 combines the traits of Number 1 (individual ego) and Number 6 (relationships, responsibility, and matters of the heart). It presents an opportunity for the individual to learn how to honor and respect love relationships responsibly and maturely, embracing their imperfections and growing from them. The key lesson is not to misuse or abuse love, avoiding leaving others confused and broken-hearted. Those with the number 16 in their charts should be cautious about the potential consequences of their actions, as the reckoning they face in the future may bring intense heartbreak and pain.

People with a 16/7 number usually exhibit the negative traits of the number 7:

- Indifference
- Analytical aloofness
- Withdrawal
- Difficult to approach
- More concern for his/ her own needs of privacy than for the feelings of others.
- Intellectualizing emotions.

The keyword for the number 16/7 is **"awaken"**: The person must awaken to the higher principles of living life on earth.

Careers for Number

Individuals with a Numerology number of 7 are often drawn to careers and fields that align with their unique qualities of analysis, introspection, spirituality, and wisdom. Whether in the realms of science, education, spirituality, or historical exploration, they contribute their intellectual and intuitive gifts to create a positive impact on society and help others navigate the complexities of life.

Explore roles like healer, historian, librarian, writer, researcher, scientist, occult practitioner, musician, or detective. Success may come in positions with spiritual authority, allowing you to share profound insights and life lessons. Sevens excel as psychiatrists, psychologists, therapists, teachers, philosophers, investigators, reporters, journalists, technicians, engineers, accountants, analysts, strategists, IT consultants, computer programmers, fitness instructors, health and wellbeing practitioners, alternative therapists, and spiritual teachers.

Compatibility of Number 7 with other Numbers

Understanding the traits and compatibility of Number 7 can provide insights into how individuals with this number may interact with others and navigate various aspects of life.

1. Spiritual and Introspective Nature:
    - Number 7 is regarded as a spiritual and introspective number.
    - It is associated with traits such as introspection, analysis, intuition, and a relentless quest for knowledge.
2. Deep and Mysterious Characteristics:
    - Number 7 is seen as a deep and mysterious number.
    - Individuals with this number are often inclined towards understanding the profound meanings of life and existence.
3. Friendly Numbers:
    - Compatible or "friendly" numbers for 7 include 4 and 7.
    - These numbers may share harmonious traits and a positive influence when interacting with 7.
4. Non-friendly Numbers:
    - Numbers considered non-friendly or less compatible with 7 are 2, 1, and 9.
    - Interactions with these numbers might pose challenges or conflicts.
5. Neutral Numbers:
    - Numbers 3, 5, 6, and 8 are considered neutral in their compatibility with 7.
    - Interactions with these numbers may not necessarily be strongly positive or negative.

Health for Number 7

Number 7 individuals often have issues related to the body, like physical weakness, as this planet has no head. They are prone to skin diseases and perspiration and are extremely sensitive to their surroundings, which at times makes them very nervous and leads to indigestion. They are easily irritated by the slightest disturbances.

They are likely to suffer from problems with the stomach, eyes, lungs, incurable diseases, and injuries to the head.

They could suffer from diseases like infection from germs, skin diseases, indigestion, gout and arthritis, nervousness, and poor blood circulation.

At a young age, they always suffer from coughs and colds, flu, congestion, tonsillitis, skin diseases, and they can also be badly affected by bad eyesight. At a later age, they can get gout and arthritis, hysteria, indigestion, and have to deal with bad blood circulation.

They should take vitamin D and E, drink fresh fruit juices, and not exhaust themselves by overworking. They should include grapes and mushrooms in their diet. Meditation is a must for these individuals.

Lucky Colours for Number 7

Numerology typically associates certain numbers with particular colors that are thought to correspond with their energy and qualities. Number 7 is considered a spiritual and introspective number associated with intuition, wisdom, and contemplation. Smoky brown or Grey Green are the most favourable colors for number 7 natives

To enhance the proper use of talents, we should wear the colours that tune with us, have those colours in our surroundings, and use those colours in day to day life.

Lucky Numbers for Number 7

Each Number is associated with certain numbers that can resonate positively with its energy. For a Life Path Number 7 individual, the numbers that often have positive significance includes:

Most Favourable Numbers: 4, 7.

Lucky Days for Number 7

Lucky Day for Number 7: Tuesday

1. Influence of Mars:
   - Tuesday is considered the lucky day for Number 7.
   - Mars, the planet associated with Tuesday, exerts its influence on individuals with the life path number 7.
2. Mars Characteristics:
   - Mars is linked to qualities such as energy, assertion, and a driving force.
   - It brings a dynamic and active energy that can align with the contemplative and analytical nature of individuals with the number 7.

Understanding the significance of Tuesday as the lucky day for Number 7 allows individuals to plan their activities and endeavours, leveraging the positive energies associated with this day.

Lucky Years for Number 7

One could consider years that correspond to the vibration of the number 7 to be fortunate. These years could include those that are numerologically significant for the number 7, such as years that reduce to 7 and 4.

To calculate the Universal Year Number, add the digits of the current year. For example, if the year is 2023, the calculation would be: 2 + 0 + 2 + 3 = 7. So, 2023 was a Universal Year 7.

Lucky years would be 2024, 2028, 2029, and 2032.

Lucky Name Number for Number 7

The total of first name and full name number should be compatible with number 7, but it should not be brought to number 7 itself.

It is to be ensured that the total of these should not be a karmic number like 16. Number 7 people can have their names at 3, 5, or 6.

Remedies for Number

a) Elemental Remedies

1. Understanding Feng Shui Elements:
   - Feng Shui, an ancient Chinese practice, associates each number with specific elements and colours.
   - Number 7 in Feng Shui is linked to the metal element.
2. Attributes of Metal Element in Feng Shui:
   - The metal element symbolizes clarity, precision, focus, and the ability to cut through obstacles.
   - It has a correlation with qualities akin to those of the number 7, such as introspection, analysis, and spiritual awareness.
3. Silver Colour Representation:
   - In Feng Shui, silver is often considered a representative colour for the metal element.
   - Silver is associated with emotional stability, intuition, and a sense of abundance.
4. Number 7 Remedy: Silver Colour Metal Strap Watch:
   - The recommendation of a silver colour metal strap watch aligns with Feng Shui principles.
   - A person's life is said to be enhanced by wearing this watch by bringing in the energy of the metal element, which is linked to the number 7.

Repetition of number 7 remedies

Repetition of number 7 more than twice can make one experience failures, betrayals, and learn from losses. The remedy for this is to avoid wearing multicoloured clothes and to donate seven grains, kajal, flag, woollen clothes, and sesame on Tuesdays.

b) Planet Remedies

Planets are associated with different numbers and their energies. Planet remedies help to balance the energies associated with the number. To balance the energy of Ketu, one must practise meditation everyday and feed black dogs. They should also worship Lord Ganesha.

c) Mantra Remedies

If positioned poorly on the chart, Ketu could cause problems for the native. Its treatments aid in protecting against negative consequences. For benefitting this planet, the mantra of Ketu should be chanted 108 times on Tuesday.

Mantra - Om Ketave Namah

d) Beej Mantra Remedies

By reciting the Navagraha Beej Mantras one can remove all malefic effects from planets. The mantra should be chanted 108 times every Tuesday.

Mantra - Aum Sram Srim Shrom Sah Ketave Namah

e) Lucky Gemstone

The gemstone for Ketu is Cat's eye chrysoberyl.

Semi-Precious Options are cat's eye quartz and cat's eye tourmaline. Wearing these stones can align the qualities of number 7. It is recommended to wear them only after the astrologer's consultation.

Bonus Section

a) Lucky Mobile Number

In numerology, every number holds a certain vibration and energy that can influence an individual's life path. Using numerological principles when deciding on a mobile number can improve luck and positive energy in one's life.

The mobile number should be friendly to root/life Path number 7. 4, 8, and 0 should be avoided as the last digit.

- If the digits in a mobile number add up to 7, it is considered to have the energy and vibrations of introspection, spiritual awareness, analytical thinking, and a quest for knowledge.
- Individuals influenced by the energy of 7 may exhibit traits such as a love for solitude, a deep need for understanding, and a contemplative nature.
- Mobile numbers totaling 7 are believed to bring positive energies associated with seeking wisdom and inner growth.
- Those with such mobile numbers might find themselves naturally inclined towards introspective activities, research, or spiritual pursuits.
- Even though the energies of the number 7 are generally pleasant, maintaining overall well-being may require striking a balance between social interaction and introspection.

b) Lucky House Number

Exploring the Significance of House Number 7:

Numerological Significance:

- In numerology, each house number carries a unique vibrational energy that can influence the experiences and dynamics within the household.

Characteristics of House Number 7:

- House number 7 is associated with the energies of introspection, spiritual awareness, and a quest for knowledge.

Homes with the number 7 may exude

- Quiet and Contemplative Atmosphere

- Spiritual Focus
- Intellectual Pursuits
- Analytical Thinking
- Study or Meditation Spaces.
- Potential Challenges:
- While the energy of 7 is often positive, it might also lead to a more introverted environment. Balancing social interactions with the need for solitude is crucial.

c) Lucky Vehicle Number

We might anticipate good fortune from our car when its number has strong fortunate vibes and is compatible with our name and birthdate. Individuals should have their vehicle number added to 1, 3, 5, or 6. Having a 7 as a total will make more religious trips, which will not benefit much.

Also, more than one 0 should be avoided in your vehicle number, as it represents the ups and downs of life.

Synopsis

In numerology, the number 7 is like a quiet philosopher, bringing a sense of introspection and spiritual awareness to those connected with it. Individuals influenced by the energy of 7 may value solitude, intellectual pursuits, and a quest for deeper knowledge. The numerology numbers associated with this number promote a balance between inner growth and practical aspects of life, making it one of the most interesting and stimulating influences.

Co - Authored by SHRRADHAA AGARWALA

THE NUMBER 8

THE NUMBER 8

*I*n Numerology, Number 8 is the most influential number and holds immense importance. It resembles the symbol of infinity. With resilience, the individual will be able to achieve great achievement and scale unimaginable heights. It's the epitome of a healthy balance. And this balance is a key factor when it comes to enduring challenges in life.

It is important as it represents balance in the spiritual and materialistic world. The symbol of 8 reflects heaven and earth in the two circles stacked on the top of each other. Number 8 very aptly represents the Proverb "As You Sow, So Shall You Reap."

Root Number 8

The people born on the 8, 17 (1+7 = 8) and 26 (2+6 = 8) are ruled and influenced by Numerology No 8. It's ruled by strong Saturn. It is the highest feminine (Yin) number.

Famous celebrities

Indian Celebrities :

1. Narendra Modi - September 17, 1950
2. Mother Teresa - August 26, 1910
3. Sourav Ganguly - July 8, 1972
4. Saina Nehwal - March 17, 1990
5. Asha Bhosale - September 8, 1933

International Celebrities :

1. Stephen Hawking - January 8, 1942
2. Benjamin Franklin - January 17, 1706
3. George Bernard Shaw - July 26, 1856
4. Larry Page - March 26, 1973
5. AB de Villiers - February 17, 1984
6. Kalpana Chawla - March 17, 1962
7. Robert Kiyosaki - April 8, 1947
8. Victor Hugo - February 26, 1802

Good Qualities of Number 8

Birth Number 8

Date of Birth: 8th of any month

Born on the 8th of any month, individuals with this birth date are ambitious warriors with a strong vision for achieving their goals. They exhibit perseverance and meticulous organization, concentrating on the minutiae of their work. They approach life's obstacles with unwavering courage and a tenacious mindset because they are resilient and patient. They take a realistic approach, put in a lot of effort to realize their goals, and give thanks to those who help them along the way. Good decision-makers with a balanced personality, embody the symbolism of number 8, represented by two zeros stacked atop each other.

Birth Number 17

Date of Birth: 17th of any month

Born on the 17th of any month, individuals with Birth Number 17 embody traits of both Number 1 and Number 7, along with the qualities of Number 8. They are individuals who are pioneers and trendsetters, motivating others to achieve their goals and embark on new beginnings. They pursue their objectives with unwavering determination, displaying courage and a strong drive. They possess analytical and intellectual abilities, value education, and possess a sharp sense of logic. With a strong intuitive faculty, they connect with divinity and receive unexpected help from the universe. Investigative by nature, they excel in technology and enjoy analyzing problems and opportunities in a careful and thorough manner.

Birth Number 26

Date of Birth: 26 of any month (2+6 = 8)

Born on the 26th of any month, individuals with Birth Number 26 inherit qualities from both Number 2 and Number 6. They value harmony, enjoying "Me Time," and pampering themselves. Intuitive and self-driven, they often navigate life guided by unseen forces. Loving and charming, they prefer winning people over with love rather than authority, striving to spread love over hatred. Supportive in tough times, they embody the saying, "A Friend in Need is a Friend Indeed." They nurture relationships and are sympathetic by nature. With a good understanding of situations and a reliable, balanced personality, Number 8 individuals are trustworthy listeners who keep secrets well.

Qualities to improve upon for Number 8

Materialistic: Their exceptional diligence and devotion never betray them and these qualities help them prosper and reach great heights. This success turned them into being much more materialistic. The people may get attracted to them for misusing and taking advantage.

Authoritative: They are very stubborn. They firmly feel that no matter what, what they are doing is correct. This increases their ego, which makes them more insensitive to the opinions of those around them. As a result, they may lose significant connections more rapidly. They become impatient and intolerant if someone contradicts them. That's why they try to hold everything in their hands or become controlling, which others dislike in them. Due to this, they may be intimidating and judgmental sometimes.

Manipulative: Success speaks itself. It's valid for Number 8. However, success also brings with it pride; if you don't keep things in check, it may ruin everything, even relationships and hard-earned money. Never do they express what's on their mind. They become secretive as they feel others are cynical. They can easily manipulate others into accepting their ideas or views.

Jealous: They have little low self-confidence. In a world filled with millions of people, they consider themselves to be aloof. Their trust in others is as thin as a snowflake, which makes them suspicious of others. This particular trait will maliciously affect their relationships, which will lead to them losing their dear ones.

Perfectionist: They are good at their work and want everyone to be good. They concentrate on minute details of their work. And expect everyone to be the same. Due to this, they become dominating, bossy, and critical. They interfere in others' work to make it perfect. They repeat the same work frequently to reach perfection. But this perfection tends to cause them to procrastinate, which delays and slows down their work.

Egoistic: Success makes them egoistic. They most likely undervalue their potential competitors once their successes get to their heads. According to them, they are the best, and others can be good or better than them, but not best. And such an attitude makes them superficial. Their conceitful nature can trivialize others' capabilities.

Ruling Planet and Qualities of Ruling Planet for Number

The number 8 ruling planet is Saturn (Shani). It is also called the Planet of Karma. Saturn is considered the judge of our good or bad karmas, which punishes or rewards us accordingly. Therefore, good deeds humans need to focus to be away from the wrath of Shani. It has a slow-moving energy that provides the virtues of justice and patience.

Saturn has the face of a complex and cruel planet. It signifies hard work and teaches many life lessons through sorrow, pain, problems, setbacks, and hurdles. That said, the period of Saturn brings you to your real purpose in life.

Saturn causes delays, dejection, disappointments, and defeats. He causes miseries, misfortunes, accidents, and sorrows. He puts obstacles in the way of progress. But, whatever it is, these obstacles are the turning point in one's life. It makes people understand the essence of their life on earth.

The Planet represents longevity. People may have a long life, as it's especially said for these people, and when someone takes their name, they come in front of them. People have to maintain balance, learn from their life lessons, and leave their lives for humanity.

Weekday ruled by Number 8

The influence of the number 8 in numerology is associated with the planet Saturn, and Saturday is considered an auspicious day for those governed by this number. Saturn, often seen as a symbol of discipline, hard work, and structure, lends its traits to individuals influenced by the number 8. Saturday, ruled by Saturn, becomes a significant day for activities, decisions, and endeavours connected to those with the energy of 8. This day is believed to enhance the positive aspects of discipline, ambition, and material success for individuals resonating with the vibrations of number 8 in numerology.

Zodiac signs for Number 8

Each individual is uniquely influenced by their ruling planet, and this connection is reflected in their behaviour and characteristics.

Two zodiac signs, Capricorn (December 22 -January 19) and Aquarius (January 20-February 18) share number 8, with Saturn as the ruling planet.

For Capricorns, the tenth astrological sign associated with Number 8, traits of perseverance, ambition, and power are prominent. The influence of Number 8 aligns with the determined and ambitious nature of Capricorns.

In the case of Aquarius, the eleventh astrological sign in the zodiac, there is a focus on the humanitarian aspect. Individuals born under this sign are driven by a desire to bring about positive change in the lives of others. The humanitarian spirit is a key characteristic associated with the influence of Number 8 on Aquarians, shaping their aspirations and actions.

Life Path Number 8

The number 8 is a symbol of balance between the spiritual and material realms, depicted by the two circles stacked on top of each other, representing heaven and earth. People associated with the number 8 are characterized by ambition, organization, practicality, and success, along with tendencies toward selfishness and materialism.

For individuals with Life Path Number 8, often considered the CEO of numerology, the shape of the number resembles the infinity sign, embodying the highs and lows of life. Eights naturally assume authoritative roles driven by their ambition, seeking leadership for financial gain or power. Eights are known for their visionary outlook, goal-oriented nature, and strong work ethic at their best. However, they can become blunt, power-hungry, and workaholics at their worst.

Let's understand with an example- Nelson Mandela, born on July 18, 1918, had a Life Path Number of 8. The Life Path Number is derived from the sum of the birth date, and in Mandela's case, it adds up to 8. Life Path Number 8 is associated with qualities such as ambition, leadership, organization, and material success. Individuals with this Life Path are often seen as powerful figures, driven by a desire for financial prosperity and authority. For Mandela, this number may have influenced his remarkable leadership qualities and his dedication to the cause of justice and equality, making a profound impact on South Africa and the world.

Careers for Number 8

As an individual with Numerology Number 8, you naturally exude power and influence, making you a magnet for success in any group. Your ability to get things done and your ambitious nature drives you to reach for the stars. Being in control is something you thrive on. When making career moves or networking, consider Wednesdays and Fridays as opportune days for interviews and connections.

Ideal career paths for you may involve roles such as CEO, builder, composer, corporate lawyer, or film producer. Other options-

1. Sports
2. Fitness
3. Lawyer
4. CEO/Supervisor/Head/Executives
5. Banking/Money/Finance
6. Business – Footwear/Oil/Sweaters/Iron
7. Land Related – Mining/Farming/Contractors-Bridges/Tenders/Flyovers/Real Estate/Wiring/Mobile Towers
8. Engineer – Mechanical/Civil/Builders
9. Occult/Spiritual Life
10. Scientist
11. Government Officials/Public Servants - Mayor, Police (any powerful position)

Compatibility of Number 8 with other Numbers

Numerological compatibility is a tool to gauge the level of agreement between individuals, assessing their suitability for various aspects such as business, relationships, or friendships. It helps examine the harmony of ideas between two people, offering insights for joint ventures or future collaborations. Different numbers exhibit varied levels of compatibility, influencing each other positively or negatively when they come together. For the number 8 in numerology:

Friendly Numbers (4, 5, 6, 8):

- These numbers generally harmonize well with 8, fostering positive interactions and mutual understanding.

Non-Friendly Numbers (1, 2, 9):

- These numbers may pose challenges or conflicts when paired with 8, requiring careful consideration and communication.

Neutral Numbers (3, 7):

- These numbers neither strongly attract nor repel 8, indicating a neutral influence in their interactions.

Numerological compatibility thus provides a nuanced understanding of how numbers influence interpersonal dynamics.

Health for Number 8

Our health is influenced by the numbers that govern us. All numbers are governed by certain planets. These planets emit rays, which have a great effect on our lifestyle and, above all, on our health.

Every number governs some part of the human body. Number 8 is dominated by the parts of the Body: Legs

Number 8 persons are normally afflicted by the following diseases:

a) Trouble with legs, shanks, teeth, and ears.
b) Arthritis, rheumatism, and gout.
c) Paralysis.
d) Frequent headaches.
e) Stomachaches, disorders of the liver and intestines.
f) Asthma, breathlessness.
g) Anaemia, Blood pressure, and Heart troubles in old age.

They should avoid any kind of intoxicant or cigarette smoke to stay well. Early rising, exercises, and breathing fresh air are essential for them to maintain their overall health.

One interesting fact about this number is that the person suffers from the ailments for a long time before getting cured.

Lucky Colours for Number 8

Black, dark blue, green, and off-white are lucky for Number 8. Even yellow, grey and purple are also favourable. They can use these colours in clothes, pillow covers, bed sheets, and wall paint.

Lucky Numbers for Number 8

In numerology, people believe that certain numbers are lucky for a person based on their birth date or name. For someone with the numerology number 8, the lucky numbers are 4, 5, 6, and 8. This means these numbers are thought to bring positive vibes or good fortune to someone with the numerology number 8. People who follow numerology may consider these numbers significant or beneficial in various aspects of life.

Lucky Days for Number 8

In numerology, some people believe that certain days of the week are luckier for individuals based on their numerology number. If your numerology number is 8, the luckiest day for you is considered to be

Saturday. Additionally, Wednesday and Friday are also seen as favourable days for people with the numerology number 8. This means that on these days, individuals with the numerology number 8 might experience positive energy or good luck, according to the beliefs of numerology enthusiasts.

Lucky Years for Number 8:

If your numerology number is 8, specific years and ages are believed to be particularly lucky for you. In the context of the Universal Year, which looks at the energy of a specific year for everyone, the fortunate years for a person with the number 8 could include 2024, 2029, 2030, and 2031.

Moreover, in terms of personal milestones, certain ages are considered auspicious for those with the numerology number 8. These include the 35th, 44th, 53rd, 62nd, 71st, 80th, and 89th years of life.

During these years, people with the number 8 might experience unexpected financial growth, career advancements, positive changes in relationships such as marriage or the birth of children, or other favourable events. These are thought to be significant periods in their lives when things are more likely to work in their favour, based on the principles of numerology.

Lucky Name Number for Number 8

Individuals with Name Number 8 are known for their strong and ambitious nature. Influenced by the qualities of the number 8, these individuals are often determined, hardworking, and goal-oriented. They possess a warrior spirit, believing in achieving their ambitions regardless of the obstacles they may encounter.

The number 8 signifies balance, and those with the name number 8 often exhibit a balanced personality. They are realistic in their approach, relying on their own efforts to achieve success.

These individuals are resilient, demonstrating strength in the face of challenges, and their decision-making abilities are noteworthy. Overall, Name Number 8 individuals are driven by a sense of purpose and possess the endurance to pursue their dreams. But because it is connected to planet Saturn, it will also bring struggle, hard work, and delays, so it is not advisable to keep a personal name number at 8.

It's good to have a Name Number for numbers 8 on 3, 5, or 6.

Remedies for Number 8

In Numerology, remedies are techniques used to balance and harmonize the higher or lower energies related with the specific number. Such remedies help to enhance the positive qualities and alleviate the challenges associated with it.

a) Elemental Remedies

Feng Shui is a Chinese practice of arranging the environment to promote harmony and balance. Each number is linked to one of the five elements in Feng Shui, and the number 8 is associated with the earth element. symbolizing stability, security, and trust.

If the Earth element is missing in your LoShu Grid, Feng Shui suggests stabilizing it by connecting with the Earth, such as by walking barefoot in a park. Feng Shui enthusiasts believe that wearing a clear quartz bracelet can help balance the energy associated with the missing number, as clear quartz is considered a powerful crystal that amplifies positive energy. Wearing this bracelet is seen as a symbolic way to bring the Earth element's energy into one's life, promoting balance and harmony according to Feng Shui principles.

Repetition of Number 8

The repetition of Number 8 in the Lo Shu Grid chart will have both negative and positive impacts. Number 8 can occur twice, thrice, four times, or even more in the Lo Shu Grid. Based on its occurrence, it affects the person's life.

- If Number 8 is coming twice in Lo Shu Grid, the person becomes stubborn and learns lessons from their own experiences. · If Number 8 is coming thrice in Lo Shu Grid, the person is inclined towards worldly pleasures and likes to buy everything that gives them happiness. They progress after the age of 40.
- If Number 8 is coming four or more times in Lo Shu Grid, they have to face life changes.
- Give away black clothes, and black blankets to the needy.
- Donate something to the service class.
- Donate mustard oil, black cloth, and Iron items - tawa, tongs, etc., on Saturday.
- Avoid wearing black clothes.

b) Planet Remedies

Number 8 is connected to the planet Saturn.

Pray Shani god or Beej mantra.

People who give you service represent Saturn; give them the profit and value of the service; reap what you sow; don't bargain with the poor; give them on time; give them money and keep some money. Keep them happy and give them rewards.

- Visit the Shani Temple on Saturdays; pour mustard oil, black whole urad, and black sesame.

Donate footwear to the poor and needy.

Worship Lord Hanuman and recite Sankatmochan, Hanuman Chalisa.

c) Mantra Remedies

Shani Mantra - Om Shanicharaya Namah - ॐ शनैचराय नमः

This above Mantra, if chanted on Saturday with full faith and devotion, one Mala of 108 Beads will help to reduce Saturn's malefic effects and gain good results. It pacifies the wrath of the Shani.

d) Beej Mantra Remedies

Shani Beej Mantra

Aum Pram Prim Prom seh Shanicharaye Namah.

ॐ प्रां प्रीं प्रौं सः शनैश्वराय नमः ॥

This Beej Mantra, if chanted on Saturday with full faith and devotion, one Mala of 108 Beads will be really helpful to overcome the problems or hurdles in life, especially in Sade Sati of Shani should chant to gain strength to face the problem and confront it bravely.

e) Lucky Gemstone

In astrology, certain gemstones are believed to be connected with specific planets. For the planet Saturn, the associated gemstone is blue sapphire. People who follow astrological beliefs may consider wearing blue sapphire to enhance the influence of Saturn in their lives.

Additionally, if Blue Sapphire isn't recommended for you, there are alternative semi-precious stones and crystals associated with Saturn. These include Amethyst, Lapis Lazuli, Clear Quartz, and Azurite. These stones are believed to have positive effects in connection with the energy of Saturn. Again, it's crucial to seek advice from an expert astrologer to determine the most suitable gemstone for your circumstances.

Bonus Section

a) Lucky Mobile Number

Mobile Number 8 is good for people who work for the masses. This number may attract wealth if you work hard. Suitable for people who are in business, education, and law.

A mobile number is considered compatible if it is friendly with the person's root number and name number.

Number 8 person can have a mobile number that has a single digit, such as 5 or 6.

b) Lucky House Number

Number 8 is perfect for those who love to dream big, are highly ambitious, and seek wealth and prosperity. You can expect sudden financial gains or a raise during your stay at a house. House number 8 is a house of power, authority, and efficiency.

House number 8 is not good for relationships. Couples who do not share a solid commitment might have a tough time in this home. The love for power leads the members to play mind-games with each other. So, it is not suitable for families.

It is very difficult to relax in this house. House number 8 can bring in power. But this house can make you morally bankrupt. One can experience legal hassles in this house. Busy schedules can prevent you from spending time with your loved ones. Occupants should take care of their health while living in the house - exercise, proper diet, and meditation are good.

c) Lucky Vehicle Number

We should avoid Number 8, as it may cause delays, accidents, or injuries. Number 8 people can have their car numbers summing to 5 and 6.

Synopsis

The number 8 is a force that can create as well as destroy. People may be either heroes or zeros. That means some will be very successful in their lives, and some will be nowhere.

Saturn will give you all the fortune and wealth you deserve. But it can bestow upon you many hardships to test you. It all depends on the judgement of your virtue and deeds. You don't get anything by luck. Number 8 are born leaders. They have a strong sense of purpose and inner drive. They are confident and assertive, and they can inspire others to follow their lead. They are not trendy, but trendsetters. They have the gift of the gab. They are success-oriented.

The number 8 represents balance and continuity in numerology. It describes a person who is ambitious and has the strength to continue in difficult times. The number 8 exudes positive energy and infinite possibilities.

Though they look tough and hard-hearted, they are soft on the downtrodden and help anyone who asks for it.

Number 8 is considered unlucky and unfavourable in Indian Numerology. It is referred to as the most intense number and brings bad omens. Saturn brings hardships, troubles, and miseries into life. It's a matter of Karma. Devastating calamities happened on Number 8. For example, the Indonesian tsunami (July 17, 2006), Kashmir earthquake (October 8, 2005), Mumbai floods (July 26, 2005), Gujarat earthquake (January 26, 2001), and the devastating Indian Ocean tsunami (December 26, 2004).

Number 8 people 'stand apart' in all aspects. They are not unlucky; they're, in fact, lucky to be different from others. There are umpteen difficult things that others can't do, but they can quite easily.

Number 8 people are special, gifted, and blessed.

Co- Authored by - Sanddhya Bhhiirud

THE NUMBER 9

THE NUMBER 9

Root Number

Those born on the 9th, 18th, or 27th of any month are ruled by the number 9. Number 9 is connected to the planet Mars in numerology.

Root number 9: -these people are generous, passionate, broadminded, compassionate, and sympathetic.

Root number 18/9: -these people are leading, courageous, innovative, self-motivated, determined and organised, strong and hardworking, and broadminded and compassionate.

Root number 27/9: - these people are harmonious, intuitive, Loving, Supportive, understanding, intellectual, investigative, analytical, technically oriented, broadminded, passionate, and generous.

Famous celebrities

Akshay Kumar (9/Sep)

Nelson Mandela (18/Jul)

Salman Khan (27/Dec),

Priyanka Chopra (18/Jul),

Suresh Raina (27/Nov)

Hima Das - January 9

Tom Hanks - July 9

Good Qualities of Number 9

People with the number 9 are described as brave, fearless, and strong. They're known for finishing whatever they set their minds to. Those with the root number 9 are punctual, like getting things done on time, and are disciplined. They prefer working independently, which makes them good at running their own businesses. However, they may not thrive in jobs where they have to take orders from others because they like having control. Number 9 is a symbol of efficient leadership, and these individuals excel when they have complete control over their work.

People with the number 9 are full of energy and power, often engaging in physical activities like going to the gym, practicing yoga, or participating in sports. They are creative and always have a desire to do something new. The interesting thing about the number 9 is that when you add any number to it, you get the same number back. For example, 9 + 2 equals 11, and 1 + 1 equals 2. This reflects how people with the number 9 treat others the way they are treated.

Those with the Root number 9 have a strong command of language but may not express their feelings quickly because they don't like appearing weak. Despite their outward strength, they have a soft heart. They often put others before themselves and actively engage in social service work, always thinking about how they can contribute to society.

People with the number 9 are straightforward and don't like beating around the bush. They speak directly, which can sometimes lead to making enemies, as not everyone appreciates their directness. These individuals live life on their terms, work hard to achieve their goals, and don't easily give up. In short, they are powerful, energetic, kind, socially conscious, and slow to forgive.

Qualities to improve upon for Number 9

People with the root number 9 are connected with the planet Mars, which is symbolized by the color red. Mars is linked to qualities like anger, power, blood, war, and energy. As a result, individuals with the root number 9 tend to get angry quickly and don't have much patience for things they consider useless. They are fearless, not afraid of anyone, and often take the lead in conflicts. They prefer not to say or hear anything wrong.

These individuals have a lot of energy inside them, and if they don't channel it in the right direction, they might find themselves in conflict. People with the Root number 9 are prone to accidents and may undergo surgery at some point in their lives. They prefer working independently, like to be in control and find it challenging to be subordinate to others.

One notable trait is that people with the Root number 9 don't forgive quickly; they may hold onto feelings of revenge. This tendency to fight can make it challenging for them to have many friends, as people might avoid interacting with them. However, once they make a friend, it tends to be a long-lasting connection.

People with the number 9 might struggle with keeping accounts in order, showing a lax approach to this aspect of life. These are areas that individuals with the number 9 may want to pay attention to and work on improving.

Ruling Planet and Qualities of Ruling Planet for Number 9

The number 9 is linked to Mars, which is like the commander-in-chief of the planets. Mars is connected with power, energy, and movement. It's described as hot, fiery, and having a masculine nature. People influenced by Mars are passionate and have the strength to achieve challenging goals. They often have good luck with matters related to land and vehicles. However, due to their aggressive and carefree nature, there's a chance they might face legal issues in life.

Those with the number 9 can be powerful forces, both for good and for not-so-good things. They are full of energy and can be a bit temperamental. It's suggested that they should be handled with discipline, love, and care. People with this number are open-hearted and speak their minds. They usually take on leadership roles among their friends. While they are honest in their dealings with friends, they can sometimes struggle with anger issues.

Weekday ruled by Number 9

For people with the numerology number 9, Tuesday is considered an auspicious day. This belief is rooted in the connection between the number 9 and the planet Mars. Each day of the week is associated with a specific planet in astrology, and Tuesday is linked to Mars.

Mars is often associated with qualities like energy, power, and assertiveness. Therefore, people with the numerology number 9, which is ruled by Mars, are thought to experience positive and favourable influences on Tuesdays. It's believed that engaging in activities, making important decisions, or starting new ventures on a Tuesday may bring about success and positive outcomes for individuals with the numerology number 9.

Zodiac signs for Number 9

Mars is a planet in our solar system, and in astrology, the number 9 has Aries (March 21 - April 19) and Scorpio (October 24 - November 22) as zodiac signs, with Mars as the ruling planet. In astrology, the zodiac is like a circle that represents the different signs, starting with Aries. Aries is often seen as the beginning of life in the zodiac, and Mars is connected with this fiery and energetic sign.

On the other hand, Scorpio is considered the last sign in the zodiac, symbolizing transformation and intensity. Traditionally, Mars is associated with both the fiery and assertive qualities of Aries at the beginning of the zodiac and the intense and transformative nature of Scorpio towards the end. So, in a way, Mars represents the journey from the lively and energetic start of life in Aries to the intense and powerful end in Scorpio in the Zodiacal circle.

Life Path Number 9

In numerology, the number "Nine" is considered the most powerful among single-digit numbers because it contains the vibrations of all the other numbers. People associated with the number nine are seen as humanitarians, caring deeply about the world. They are natural leaders, although they don't actively seek out leadership roles; it tends to happen naturally for them. Nines are idealistic and often lend their support to worthwhile social causes.

At their best, nines are selfless, compassionate healers. However, at their worst, they can be emotionally distant, resentful, and complex. Nines are known for their bravery and courage, easily adapting to different circumstances and showing endurance. They are determined, and aggressive, and they won't stop until they achieve their goals. Despite having a strong temper, they lead fulfilling married lives, love children, and prioritize family.

Describing them as hot, fiery, dynamic, fast, and male, Nines possess qualities like activity, courage, enthusiasm, energy, and sensuality. They are practical, inventive, scientific, responsible, tactful, diplomatic, and have sound judgement and strong intuition. Nines can be philosophical with artistic tendencies, expressing themselves well in speech and writing. Women with the number nine are often good and efficient at practical tasks, like kitchen work. Overall, Nines are characterized by fire, anger, passion, penetration, power, enterprise, and a strong sense of family.

Careers for Number 9

Since the number 9 is connected to the fire element, individuals with this number can excel in jobs related to fire, such as working in hotels, restaurants, as chefs, or in other fire-related fields. They have a lot of energy, making them well-suited for sports and fitness. Additionally, they thrive in creative fields like acting and can even engage in creative writing projects. If they choose, they can be outstanding athletes.

People with the number 9 possess a clear vision and know how to use their strengths in important situations, making them excellent leaders. Their strong sense of justice makes them suitable for careers as lawyers or social workers. Given their patriotic nature, they may also pursue careers in the army or military. Professions like technicians (especially in electronics), doctors, and chemists are also well-suited for them.

Individuals with the root number 9 are known for their energy, power, and ability to do various types of work. They excel in fields that require enthusiasm for social service, such as working for NGOs, the military, the Air Force, police, and army officers. They also perform exceptionally well in the medical field, as surgeons or dentists. Since root number 9 is associated with the fire element, careers in hotels, restaurants, and as chefs suit them well. Politics is another area where they shine due to their leadership skills. Sports and fitness, as seen in individuals like PT Usha and Suresh Raina, and the acting field, as seen in stars like Akshay Kumar, Salman Khan, and Priyanka Chopra, are also excellent fits for people with the root number 9.

Compatibility of Number 9 with other Numbers

In numerology, compatibility is often assessed based on the inherent qualities associated with each number and how they align or clash in personal and professional relationships.

1. Number 9 is compatible with 1, 3, and 9:

- Reasons:
  - 1: Both 1 and 9 have qualities associated with leadership and authority. Number 1 represents fatherhood and leadership, and when combined with 9, there's a harmonious alignment of these characteristics.
  - 3: The number 3 is associated with creativity and communication. 9 and 3 complement each other well, as 9 brings a sense of vision and 3 adds creativity, making it a harmonious pairing.
  - 9 (Self-Compatibility): Being compatible with oneself means that the person tends to understand and resonate with their own qualities. In this case, the characteristics associated with 9 align well with each other.
2. Number 9 is not compatible with 2, 4, 5, 6, or 8:
   - Reasons:
     - 2: Number 2 is often associated with cooperation and diplomacy, which may clash with the more assertive and independent nature of 9.
     - 4 and 9 (Not Complementary in Personal Relationships): The practical and disciplined nature of 4 may clash with the idealism and visionary approach of 9 in personal relationships.
     - 5: 5 is associated with freedom and change, which may clash with the more stable and routine-oriented nature of 9.
     - 9 and 6 (Conflict in Relationship): The nurturing and harmonizing nature of 6 may conflict with the independent and visionary approach of 9.
     - 7: 7 is analytical and introspective, while 9 is more outward-focused and visionary, leading to potential misunderstandings.
     - 8: 8 is often associated with power and authority, and the independent nature of 9 may resist being controlled or directed by 8.
3. Specific Pairings:

9 and 7 (Complementary): Complementary numbers often balance each other. Here, the intuitive and spiritual nature of 7 complements the visionary and humanitarian qualities of 9.

9 and 9 (Good in Business): While personal compatibility may be challenging, both being 9s in a business setting can work well due to shared qualities of leadership, vision, and determination.

Health for Number 9

People with the root number 9 in their numerology profile often face health issues related to blood, such as low blood pressure (low BP) or high blood pressure diseases. If a person has the root number 9 appearing more than twice in their Lo Shu grid, they might be more prone to accidents and may even undergo surgery at some point in their life.

The reason behind this is that the number 9 is ruled by Mars, which is associated with themes like battlefields, accidents, injuries, and blood. The number 9 signifies aggression, passion, and energy, which can contribute to health issues such as stress, blood pressure problems, kidney control, various types of fever, throat issues, and bronchitis. Additionally, the number 9 is connected to accidents and injuries for individuals with this root number.

Lucky Colours for Number 9

For individuals with the numerology number 9, colours like red and pink are considered suitable. This is because the number 9 is associated with the planet Mars, often referred to as the red, fiery planet. The connection between the number 9 and Mars makes red and pink colours resonate well with the energy and qualities linked to this number.

Wearing red and pink is thought to align with the characteristics of Mars, which include traits like passion, energy, and assertiveness. These colours are believed to enhance the positive aspects associated with the number 9.

Additionally, individuals with the number 9 can also consider wearing the colour yellow. While not directly related to the red fiery nature of Mars, yellow is associated with attributes like warmth, brightness, and energy. It can complement the qualities of the number 9, adding a vibrant and positive touch to their overall aura.

Lucky Numbers for Number 9

The lucky numbers 1, 3, and 9 are considered fortunate for individuals with the numerology number 9 due to their alignment with qualities like leadership, creativity, communication, and the inherent positive energy associated with the number 9 itself. These numbers are thought to enhance the overall luck and positive outcomes in various aspects of the lives of individuals with the number 9.

Lucky Days for Number 9

Tuesday, Sunday, and Thursday are considered lucky days for individuals with the numerology number 9 due to their associations with the planets Mars, the Sun, and Jupiter, respectively. Engaging in activities on these days is believed to enhance positive energies and outcomes for individuals with the number 9.

Lucky Years for Number 9

In numerology, the Universal Year is determined by adding the digits of the current year to get a single-digit number, influencing everyone with an overall energy or theme. Specifically, the years 2025, 2026, 2028, 2030, and 2034 are deemed advantageous for those with the numerology number 9 for the following reasons:

1. 2025 (Universal Year 9): The year's energy aligns with the number 9, emphasizing humanitarianism, leadership, and completion.

2. 2026 (Universal Year 1): While not a Universal Year 9, the transition to 2026 as a Universal Year 1 signifies new beginnings, independence, and leadership, complementing the traits of number 9 individuals.
3. 2028 (Universal Year 3): This year offers opportunities for creative expression, effective communication, and positive social connections for those with the numerology number 9.
4. 2034 (Universal Year 9): Similar to 2025, this year aligns with the energy of the number 9.

In summary, these years are considered beneficial for numerology number 9 individuals due to the alignment of the Universal Year's energy with the inherent qualities of the number 9.

Lucky Name Number for Number 9

If you have the name number 9, you are likely to have a strong feeling of attaining an influential position in society. They are patient by nature and are able to ward off any kind of trouble in their lives through courage and hard work. Number 9 is a beneficial soul number for politicians, athletes, those in the military, artists, musicians, and even those dedicated to leading more spiritual lives.

Remedies for Number 9

a) Elemental Remedies

If number 9 is missing in your chart, then wear a red thread on any hand. Keeping a picture of a fire or a red bulb in the south direction can be helpful.

If number 9 is repeated more than twice, then You should donate red things like jaggery, red lentils, red cloth, copper, and red sweets to poor people on Tuesday.

b) Planet Remedies

- Hanuman Chalisa should be recited every Tuesday.
- Donating blood as per your wish is also a great donation.
- Exercise should be done for at least 15 to 20 minutes daily.

c) Mantra Remedies

Chanting the mantra "Om Bhaumaya Namah" 108 times is a spiritual practice in Vedic astrology.

Mars, associated with energy and courage, is believed to be strengthened through this mantra. The repetition aligns personal energy with Mars, promoting empowerment, resilience, and astrological balance. This devotional practice aims to foster a harmonious connection with the planetary influence, enhancing overall well-being.

d) Beej Mantra Remedies

To make Mars powerful in a person's chart, this Beej Mantra should be chanted 11, 27, 51, and 108 times. This is the mantra! Om Kram Kreem Kraum Sah Bhaumay Namah.

e) Lucky Gemstone

Number 9 in numerology is governed by the planet Mars (Mangal Grah), and accordingly, the red coral gemstone, known as "Moonga," is considered beneficial for individuals with this numerology.

The red coral is believed to enhance the positive influences of Mars, fostering qualities such as energy, courage, and assertiveness.

However, it's crucial to note that the use of red coral should be done under the guidance of an experienced astrologer.

Bonus Section

a) Lucky Mobile Number for number 9

If an individual is actively involved in social, political services, sports, or physical activities, having the number 9 as their mobile number is considered auspicious. Numerology number 9 people can also use a total of 1 or 3 as their mobile number.

b) Lucky House Number for number 9

The number 9 holds profound symbolic significance, representing humanitarianism and tradition. In the realm of numerology, individuals associated with the number 9 are often characterized by their compassionate and altruistic nature.

Similarly, when considering house numbers, the number 9 is believed to be particularly advantageous for those actively engaged in social and political pursuits or the entertainment industry. The vibrational energy of the number 9 aligns well with the qualities required for impactful contributions in these fields.

Living in a house with the number 9 may enhance the resident's ability to foster positive social change, uphold traditional values, and thrive in creative and entertaining endeavors. This alignment is rooted in the belief that the energy associated with the number 9 can complement and amplify the pursuits of individuals deeply involved in social, political, or entertainment-related activities.

c) Lucky Vehicle Number

Number 9 denotes red colour. A normal person should avoid it because it shows aggression and energy in the color, but in the sports industry, for racing cars, the color red is very suitable. A person should avoid using the number 9 as a vehicle number or the repetition of the number on the number plate because there are chances of accidents. However, exceptions can be made for politicians, actors, NGOs, officers, doctors, etc., if the total sum, including relevant taxes, equals 9.

Synopsis

Numerology number 9 is characterized by its association with humanitarianism, compassion, and leadership. Individuals with this number are often driven by a strong desire to make positive contributions to society.

They possess natural leadership qualities, displaying courage, assertiveness, and a visionary outlook. The number 9 is symbolic of completion and unity, representing the culmination of spiritual growth.

Those influenced by this number are drawn to social and political endeavours, thriving in roles that allow them to make a meaningful impact. The energy of Mars governs the number 9, connecting it to qualities like energy, passion, and assertiveness. Additionally, the number 9 is linked to the fire element in Feng Shui, reinforcing its dynamic and transformative nature.

People with the numerology number 9 may find fulfillment in creative pursuits, social service, and leadership roles, embodying the essence of a compassionate and influential individual.

Co-Authored by - Shillpa P Chinchole and Meenakkshi

CONCLUSION

*I*n "Numbers Do Wonders," we explored the profound impact of numerology on our lives and how understanding the power of numbers could transform destinies.

It unveiled the idea that each number held unique energies influencing various aspects of existence, from career and health to wealth and relationships.

The book illustrated how numbers served as guides, revealing insights into personalities, strengths, and challenges. Emphasizing the wisdom of numerology, it empowers individuals to make informed decisions, navigate challenges, and harness positive energies associated with their unique numbers.

Through real-life examples and practical guidance, "Numbers Do Wonders" inspired readers to tap into the magic of numerology, allowing them to chart a course toward a fulfilling and harmonious life across all dimensions.

Think of numerology not just as a tool but as a way to understand the patterns of the universe and where we fit into it. I hope the things you've learned from this book help you face life's challenges and welcome its opportunities with a clearer understanding.

By:- Jhhilmil M Shah (Maestro Of Numerology)

Connect with us @ Metavalley

www.ingramcontent.com/pod-product-compliance
Lightning Source LLC
LaVergne TN
LVHW041707070526
838199LV00045B/1249